HEROES
UNDER THE BIG DIPPER

A TRUE STORY

Author Peter LaCivita -- United States Marines
December 1942-November 1945

Fleet Marine Force - Pacific

U.S. MARINES

Author: Peter LaCivita

Library of Congress Catalog Card Number: 97-94028
ISBN: 1-57502-539-6

Printed in the USA by

3212 East Highway 30 • Kearney, NE 68847 • 1-800-650-7888

DEDICATION

To my wife, Gilda

My children: Judie, Robert, and Thomas

And my grandchildren: Deena, Gregory, Christina, Bradley, Marc, and Bryan

And all future generations

ACKNOWLEDGMENTS

I would like to acknowledge the Marines of the twenty Defensive Battalions which comprised the foundation of the U.S. Marine Corps. These men withstood all the elements of the Pacific, including heat that sometimes reached 130 degrees F.; twenty-six continuous days of rain; Monsoon weather; mosquitoes; thousands of rats, land crabs, large flies, snakes, and even the monitor lizard. I extend my thanks especially to the men of the Tenth Defensive Battalion and the Seventh Anti-aircraft Battalion Fleet Marine Force (a part of the First and Fifth Marine Amphibious Corps.)

Most of these men were in their teens at the time and had never been away from home before. My experiences were also their experiences. We shared good times, bad times, heat, sweat, laughter, and sadness.

Although the events and instances of which I wrote took place over fifty years ago, they are all to the best of my knowledge, true. None of the men which I identify are fictional.

My deepest thanks to my daughter, Judie Schneider and to Professor Fiori Pugliano for their practical suggestions and proofreading skills.

And especially, I would like to thank the Lord God Almighty who watched over me and gave me His Word while boarding ship -- "Be strong, and of good courage. Be not afraid... For the Lord thy God is with thee...."

Foreword

They came from Brooklyn, San Francisco, Denver, Chicago, Detroit and Pittsburgh, from the shores of New Jersey to farmlands of Kansas, from the mountains of Colorado to the plains of Montana. From every state, from every major city, from every walk of life, and from every religion. They were marines, soldiers, sailors, coast guard men; they were SPARS, WAVES and WACS; they were farmers, laborers, bricklayers, nurses, doctors and lawyers and even Indian Chiefs; over 16 million men and women fought for the US in World War II.

Life during this conflict shifted from lonely to boring, from cold to hot, from rain to drought. The war itself was dull, but with many moments of stark terror. American men and women fought all over the world from North Africa to New Guinea, from the beaches of Normandy to the sands of Iwo Jima, from the Aleutian Islands to the Philippines.

Some of the hardest fighting of the war took place in the South Pacific by the men of the US Marine Corps. Among the men who fought the long hard war in this area was Peter LaCivita, an average "Joe Six-Pack" from East McKeesport, PA. This is his story. It is full of humor and anecdotes and tells of the horrors of real fighting, of the good time and the bad, of sadness and laughter, of men who went to war as young teenagers--just kids--and returned men. It was not the generals like MacArthur, Bradley, Ridgeway, or Eisenhower who won the war but the foot soldier "GI Joe," the Navy "swabee," the Marine "gyrene." It was a doughboy's war.

This story, written over fifty years after the war, is the same for all who served and the reader can relate to what happened to Mr. LaCivita. In a way it is not his story but the story of everyone who fought and died so that the evil Hitler, Mussolini and Tojo could be defeated.

While Mr. LaCivita dedicates this book to those who served with him, the Marines of the Twenty Defensive

Battalions, I would add that is also dedicated to the over 16 million Kilroys who served and who were there. It is a story that all who have ever been to war can relate to. May we never forget, and as the Marines so proudly say "semper Fi."

Donald M. Goldstein, 1997
Pittsburgh, PA
(author of 18 books including *Miracle At Midway, At Dawn We Slept, Pearl Harbor,* and *Amelia Earhart - A Centennial Biography)*

Heroes Under the Big Dipper

I never quite believed I was in a war until that morning on an American liberty ship. We were just three days out from New Caledonia. As we spotted land up ahead, one of my Marine buddies said it was Guadalcanal. We kept moving closer until we anchored three miles out at sea. Then with a shout my best friend—Bill Lawrence—and I were ordered along with only ten other Marines to pick up our gear, climb down the nets and get into the Higgins boat to take us to shore. Looking back at our newly made friends on the ship, we never had time to say goodbys as the Higgins landed on shore near the airstrip of the island.

There wasn't anyone around! No one to tell us where to go, or what to do. Everything looked deserted. My ankle was killing me. Having sprained it in a tackle football game in New Caledonia, I removed the wrap around my ankle to find my whole foot swollen. I sat to re-wrap it, when I heard a truck barreling up the beach toward us.

The driver stopped the truck and started screaming, "Quick! Pick up your gear and get on the truck! Get the hell out of here!" He recklessly drove us into a wooded area about one hundred yards away, and shouted, "Get off NOW! Find yourself a foxhole!"

Suddenly we heard planes in the sky approaching with a roar. We scattered. Four of us came upon the same foxhole and we were still trying to figure out how four guys would get into one foxhole, when search lights lit up the sky. We could see the tracers from the .50-caliber machine guns. The 20mm, 40mm, and 90mm guns started booming away.

As we stood there, watching what looked like fireworks back home on the Fourth of July, someone said, "Wow! It's just like in the movies!"

Right then, a Japanese zero flew above the treetops. The four of us dove into one foxhole, one on top of the other. I landed on top, facing the sky. What a sight it was—searchlights on the zero while planes almost skimmed the coconut trees! We heard a deafening boom and popped our heads out the hole to see something burning out at sea. By golly, the planes had made a direct hit on our American liberty ship! I never realized that a ship with all that metal could burn so quickly. The ship became red hot as the fire raged until the ship eventually went under.

We didn't get any sleep that night. Seeing bodies floating onto the shore the next morning, we wondered if anybody had survived. For the rest of the day, no one came around to give the twelve of us any directions. We were just left with our thoughts on a beautiful, seemingly deserted Pacific island. It was August 12, 1943.

chapter 1

"I'd Rather Be Poor In America."

I was born in a small town named Wilmerding. It sat in a broad valley surrounded by Wall and Turtle Creek and various other strangely named hamlets which sat 16 miles east of Pittsburgh, Pennsylvania. My parents immigrated to Wilmerding from Italy after World War I. My dad's grandparents were immigrants from Italy to Argentina many years before, so my Grandma LaCivita and my dad were born in Buenos Aires. When my dad was a youngster, his family moved back to Bovino, Italy. Before World War I my dad was given a choice to either join the Italian Army or go back to Argentina. He chose to fight. After the war he operated a small business selling solid fuel used for heating and cooking stoves.

My mom came from Foggia, Italy. Her family, consisting of three brothers and twin sisters, was well to do compared to my dad's family. Her father owned a block of houses and was in the export business. They lived in luxury with a house maid, a cook and ground keepers. Despite the families' financial differences, because my mother's and father's families were friends, they made a marriage match between my dad, Giovanni, and Valardina, my mom. Their first child, Peter, died after one year. In the "old country" it was a tradition to name your children after a brother or sister, and Peter, was my dad's oldest brother. Their second child was my sister, Lucille. By now the economy was bad in Italy and living conditions were becoming poor. My parents packed up Lucille, said goodby to their families, and headed for the country of "milk and honey"—America. They settled in Wilmerding and there I was born, named after my older brother who had died.

Jobs were plentiful to the immigrants during the "Roaring Twenties." Dad chose to work at the Pennsylvania Railroad Pitcairn yards. Work was steady so he bought a house on a hill overlooking the Wilmerding valley in a small town called East McKeesport. One year later my brother, Louie, was born; two years later, Mary; then came Josephine, Tony, Margaret, and Michael; all born in the house on top of the valley. When my oldest sister, Lucille, was 12 years old, she and I became the family baby sitters. I'll never forget how she cried while my mother gave birth to Baby Michael. "Enough is enough," she cried, "Pete and I will never have time for ourselves." During this last pregnancy my mother was bedfast for three months and the burden was on our shoulders to take care of the family while dad was at work. We missed many days of school and that was all I needed! It was tough enough for both of us because in first grade we couldn't speak a word of English—"but, oh, good Italian!" My friend, Stanley Zywar was Polish and he couldn't speak English—"but, oh, good Polish." So we had a language of our own and somehow we understood each other perfectly. Our communication was as spontaneous and natural as a mother with her child. Likewise we were amazed how my mother who spoke broken English could sit talking to Mrs. Praisner from Poland, who spoke broken English. They could sit for hours talking to each other and no one could understand a word of their conversation.

In the 1930's, times started getting rough. Work everywhere slowed and my dad kept getting laid off from the railroad. We went on welfare rolls and for many families on our hill welfare consisted of a clothing voucher. You took this voucher to a designated store, and were given shoes that were either too big or too small, and clothes that could only fit "if you grew fast." In school you knew who was on welfare by the way their clothes fit them. Food distribution consisted of butter, cheese and a sack of flour. I recall when my dad found work, on payday he'd come home with cream puffs. We couldn't wait for payday! At times my mom couldn't wait for my dad to come home from work. On those particular days, I, though only nine years old, as the oldest son, was given the responsibility to pick up his pay. We lived on the top of a steep hill overlooking Wilmerding, where I would catch a trolley car to Pitcairn to meet my dad at the gate at 10 o'clock in the morning. On this hillside had been built 100 steps through the woods which I would gallop down on my way to get the trolley to meet my dad. He would then pin his pay in my pocket and order me to go straight home. I would then catch the trolley back and run up those 100 steps with the money. Then I had the privilege of going with my mother to the grocery store.

In the spring, my mother and I would go to the open fields on the hillside and pick dandelions, wild broccoli, elderberries, edible mushrooms and greens. Sometimes I'd feel a bit embarrassed walking through town with a large basket full of greens, but I knew with those greens my mom would make the most delicious meal, accompanied with her homemade bread.

Somehow my mother was able to manage with what little we had. Weeks before a holiday it seemed she made bushels of various cookies spending long hours in the kitchen. It was heartbreaking for her though when she would hang up our stockings on Christmas Eve. At the bottom of each was a dime we could use for a movie, along with an apple, orange and a candy bar. The girls had a doll hanging out of their stockings and every year the boys found a new mouth organ in theirs. Dad would then place under the tree a special piece of clothing for each of us. Holidays, despite the scarce times, remained joyous.

My mother at this time made most of my sister's clothes, so we purchased a Singer Sewing Machine. It was on the "easy payment plan." I'll never forget the day two men came to the house to repossess the sewing machine because my mom missed a payment. My dad wasn't home at the time, so the two men picked it up and started to carry it from the dining room. Mom started to cry and when the children saw her crying we initiated a tug-of-war between the two men on one end of the machine and my brother, two sisters, and me on the other. My little brother, Louie, ran down the basement and came up with a hatchet and started chopping on the men's feet. They both left go of the machine and ran out of the house. They never came back to get the sewing machine again.

Louie was a tough little kid. When he was six years old, we all had attended a wedding in the next town. After the wedding it was late and the street cars were finished running for the night, so my dad called for a taxicab. In those days the cab had a jump seat which would fold down and was behind the front seat. My brother, Louie and I argued about who would sit on that jump seat, which was near the door. Lou won. The road home had street car tracks on it and wound around a large hill for four miles. We all dozed off and when we reached our house, we saw mother look around, suddenly become frantic, and scream, "Louie! Where is my Louie?" Sure enough, Lou was missing. My dad checked Lou's side of the door. It was loosely closed, so we assumed he must have fallen out. Everyone got back into the cab. The driver was just as concerned as we were, so he backtracked. About halfway down the hill, I saw two feet hanging over a ditch. They were not moving. "Stop!" I cried, "there he is, Dad." My mother kept screaming, "Oh, my poor Louie!" When my dad got out, he picked him up, and by golly, Lou was sleeping soundly. He never knew that he had fallen out of the taxi door and into a ditch. That's just the kind of kid he was.

All of us had a special chore to do around the house except for Louie. My job was cleaning up the kitchen, so twice a week I would scrub the kitchen floor. One Saturday I had just mopped the floor when in comes Louie with muddy shoes. He always wore a hat that he would paint a different color every week. My mop was still soaking in the bucket, so I picked it up and hit him over the head. His hat, brittle from too much paint, broke into two pieces with the rim falling down over his ears. He ran out of the house laughing, while I had to scrub the mess his muddy shoes and painted hat had left on the floor.

We used to get spankings from my dad when we didn't behave, so all my mother had to say was, "Wait until your dad comes home from work," and all eight of us would straighten up. The angriest I ever saw my father was when my friends and I got caught stealing grapes from Mr. Schantz's vines. He told my dad, and my sister warned me before I got home that I was "in for it." My dad didn't need a strap. Dad was a blacksmith on the railroad now and his hands were tough. I loafed around the street afraid to go into the house that day. I missed supper and dad started calling, "Pete, I want to talk to you." Making my move, I ran into the house and hid under the bed. My dad, trying to get me, kept moving from one end of the bed to the other. As this went on over and over again, he became more agitated. Finally, furious with me, he literally took the bed apart, grabbed me, put me over his knee, and made my rear end pretty sore. He then gave me a lecture and asked me how I would like it if someone would steal our corn or tomatoes after we worked so hard to grow them. He warned me never to steal again and in the same breath told me to go down and eat my supper.

One day Dad had just brushed a coat of tar on our front porch roof. Louie and I decided it would be a great idea to crawl out the bedroom window onto the roof and give it "the once over." We were covered with black tar, standing on the roof, when just then my dad sticks his head out the window and orders us to get back into the house. "No, Dad," we said, "You're going to spank us."

"No, no," my dad replied, "I'm going downstairs. Don't worry, come back into the house."

I then told Lou to stick his head into the window to see if Dad was anywhere in sight. Lou poked his head back into the window, and I gave him a big push, tumbling him into the room. Hearing my dad's voice proclaim, "Now I got you!", I jump through the window, pass Louie in my dad's hold, and run out of the house! I waited that night until my dad went to bed before I went back. He got up early for work and I never did get punished for that one. When I reached 10 years old my dad told me I was too old to be spanked, and hoped by now that I knew the difference between right and wrong. My dad expected a little more from me being the oldest son.

When I was twelve years old, I started delivering newspapers. Finally I earned enough money to make monthly payments on a new refrigerator. How happy my mother was the day it was delivered! Mother bragged about my accomplishment for years.

I knew my dad was a good example for me. He was proud to be an American citizen as was my mother. She used to say, "I was rich in Italy, but I'd rather be poor and live in the United States." An array of families of many different nationalities lived on our hill. The hill we lived on was called "the Terrace." It existed of about 30 houses filled with families from many nations. There was a Russian family, African-American family, Dutch, Polish, English, Irish, German, Lituanian, Italian and Slovak families. When Germany invaded Italy, and Italy became part of the Axis, three neighbors—Nucci Severinio, Mr. Howard and Mr. Lancaster got into a "friendly" discussion about the situation. Nucci didn't like some of the things that were being said about his native land -- Italy, and he defended its people. Mr. Lancaster made the remark that Nucci wasn't acting like a "good American." Nucci, to prove him wrong, took paint and painted the slats of the siding on his house red, white, and blue until the whole house looked like an American flag. He then attached a sign to it which read -- "Now who is the best American on the hill?"

When I was in tenth grade my neighbor bought a set of weights and talked me and Louie into starting a weight lifting club. I was always one of the smaller boys in school until I grew taller when I was a junior, so I met and worked out three times a week in a neighbor's garage which we named the Terrace Gym. We were then called "the nuts" by our elders. Weight lifting was not very popular. They said we would be muscle bound by the time we were thirty. By eleventh grade I was ready to display weight lifting fundamentals in one of our Friday assemblies at school. After that day I was nicknamed "Weight lifter." We felt we were pioneers in our area following Bob Hoffman of York, Pennsylvania, known as "the Father of Weight lifting." In the Terrace Gym we faithfully did our exercises three times a week. Louie, however, very seldom showed up to exercise. When he did, he either matched my effort or lifted a few more pounds than I. He seemed to gain strength without even lifting.

One day as a teen, he and his friend, Joe Tucci, tried to beat the Capitol Limited Train across the tracks which used to run through McKeesport at twelve o'clock every night. One night their bumper got caught on the engine and dragged their car for five blocks before it unhooked itself. They both walked away without a scratch, leaving the car and never going back to it. Louie went on during World War II to France to fight with Patton's army. He just seemed to have an "angel on his shoulder."

I graduated from East McKeesport High School. After graduation I could not afford to go to college. My dad, who now worked for the Pennsylvania Railroad, suggested I apply for a machinist's apprenticeship. I applied, took the appropriate exam, and within two weeks was notified that I was one of two accepted for a four-year apprenticeship. Dad was very proud of me. The starting salary of thirty cents per hour would increase by five cents every six months. I liked the job on the railroad cleaning engines and tenders. We had class every morning and worked in the engine with the engineers. Though all the engines then ran by coal and coke, most of our schooling prepared us for the new diesel engines still on the drawing board. We were given the night shift for one month and had the job of pumping hard grease into the engine wheels. The grease had to be fed with pressure by hand into the grease gun, so as most railroad jobs, it was extremely hard work.

Now that I had a steady job, I decided to buy a car. I purchased 1933 Plymouth sedan from a used car dealer for $35.00. It was on the "easy payment plan." What a bargain! Now I could go on a date with my own wheels. My friend Steve Huchrowski, whom I called "Hookers," and I decided to go on a double date. We planned to go to Kennywood Park—the largest amusement park in the area. The skies appeared cloudy and overcast that day, but we decided to go anyway. Half way to the park in the Plymouth, it started to rain. Hookers was in the back seat with his date, and mine was up front with me. We were singing along with the radio when a few drops of rain came through the Plymouth's roof. Suddenly, it started leaking so badly, there was no place in the car to keep dry. What was I to do? Then I saw a variety store ahead. I stopped the car, ran in and purchased two umbrellas. My date held an open umbrella up front and Hooker's date held one open in the back. We laughed the rest of the evening, even though our clothes were wet. After that day, I always kept two umbrellas in the car. It was embarrassing when I drove my parents in the car when it rained. I can still picture my mother holding an umbrella over my dad as they sat in thc back seat while I chaperoned them in my Plymouth. I didn't keep that car too long. I purposely missed a few "easy payments" until the day a tow truck came to take it away.

I had been an apprentice for six months and my hourly rate climbed to 35 cents an hour, when we heard that a place called Pearl Harbor had been attacked. Most of us had never heard of this place, but the news of American lives lost on our ships and the way the attack was carried out gave me an uneasy feeling. Shortly after that, a place called Wake Island was overrun. Now at work we were doing more manual work as freight and troop trains were being placed into use. The Battle of Midway was building up.

My apprentice friend quit when he discovered he could make more money in the steel mill. The more I thought about the war, the more I knew I would never finish my apprenticeship. I asked my dad how he would feel if I left the railroad for the service. He advised me to consult with the main office and suggest a temporary release from my apprenticeship until after the war. They said they wouldn't hear of it, so I left the railroad and got a better paying job at the Westinghouse Airbrake working in their machine shop.

Dad knew I would be leaving for the service soon. He was in World War I and had fought in France. He understood how I felt. At this time my hometown friends, Ed VonKrug, the Tucci boys, and I made the best of it almost every night down in my basement with the barrels of homemade wine. My dad permitted us to draw from the barrels any time as long as none of us ever left the house. We always obeyed that order. My dad thought it better we drink at home rather than in bars.

There were times though when we had unexpected weekday visitors. When the main water lines would freeze up in the front street, the water company workers had to hook up a welder to the water line. For some reason they always hooked it up in our cellar, where all the wine was. It always took a few days for the lines to thaw. Those workers went home feeling pretty good every day. They appreciated our cellar, and we always got a bargain on our water bill.

In November 1942, gasoline started to be rationed. Our traveling was limited and items such as meat, potatoes, sugar, and butter became scarce. Our home front set up a civilian guard system and air raid drills became a common event. When the air raid siren blasted all traffic stopped and all lights were turned off. Most homes had black window blinds so no light could be seen from the outside. Each civilian guard was assigned a certain area to patrol and enforce the "lights outs." I never understood why the guard walked around with a flashlight. Couldn't he be seen? When the "all clear" signal was given, lights were permitted back on. I felt that these drills managed to "scare the hell" out of young children, but did little else.

Most of our friends had either been drafted into the Army or enlisted into the Navy. My friend, Hooker, and I decided to join rather than be drafted. So on December 11, 1942, we walked into the Marine station located in downtown Pittsburgh to enlist. You filled out the recruitment papers and had your physical that same day. Our recruitment officer was A.E. Simon. We were in good shape and passed with flying colors. Not everyone had it so easy. One recruit was told he was one pound overweight. If he could lose that pound, he would be accepted. They suggested he run around the block and then get back on the scale. He did just that! He ran around the block, came back huffing and puffing, and got on the scale a second time. They laughed, and told him, "You did it!"

Thirty in our group were sworn in that day. There was no backing out now. We were instructed to go home, straighten things there, and to report to the YMCA that next evening carrying only toiletries and one extra pair of socks and underwear.

When I got home that day, I sat my mom down and told her that I had just joined the Marines. She started to cry. "Mom, why are you crying?" I asked. "You knew I was gong into the service."

"Why did you join the submarine?" she asked, "I'll worry every day while you're under the water."

"No, mom," I said, "The Marines have nothing to do with the submarines. They are just called Marines. Duties are the same as the Army except that they are better trained." After this explanation she felt much better.

chapter

From Boys to Men

That evening Steve and I said goodbye to our families and reported to the YMCA. The Marine in charge of our group told us that we could roam the city that night, but that he didn't want to see any of us "loaded," and we had to be in by eleven o'clock. He told us that we were by no means full-fledged Marines, so we shouldn't go around acting tough. We all made it through that night without incident, and the next morning we were "marched" to the train station. The train had a special coach just for us. We also had our own dining car which we shared with other Marines who had enlisted. The coach was full, and we were headed south for Parris Island, S.C. The coach was very noisy, because the big thing to do was crap shooting. The seats on the train were made in such a way that you could push the back so that four people could face one another. Besides my friend Hookers, I met other recruits: Chorba, Havko, Ried, and Fuelmer. All began encouraging me, "Come on get into this crap game!" I knew nothing about dice.

"Here's the dice, put a dollar into the pile and roll 'em!"

I rolled the dice and up comes a seven. "You won!" They threw more money on the pile. I roll and up comes another seven! "You won again!" More money was thrown into the pile. Others were exchanging money. Now I haven't the faintest idea what I'm doing, but I roll again. Up comes four on me and four on the other. "Come on, you can do it. You've a hot hand," they shout. I shake the dice in my hand, throw, and up comes four on one and four on the other. "You did it!" they cried. Though I had no idea what I had done or how I managed to do it, I won $76.00, big money in those days. Despite, myself, I felt something or someone special was looking out for me.

When we were delayed in Washington, D.C., instead of us being allowed to get off the train, our coaches, including our dining car, were just hooked onto another train. This seemed to be the policy every time we transferred. But we didn't mind. The food was tops and the Marine Corps was sure doing it up right!

Early in the morning on December 13, 1942, we pull into Beaufort, S.C. As I step off the train, I'm impressed with the stunning contrast from home. The palm trees and flowers still in bloom, though beautiful, gave me a homesick feeling. Everything around me, so different from the wintery landscape of home, only made me feel so very far away from the home I loved.

"OK, you civilians, form a double line, face those trucks. I want you on those trucks and no talking," a Sergeant ordered. The trucks were big old military trucks that looked like cattle cars. There were no seats in the truck and we had to stand. Throughout the drive the Sergeant insulted us, "You're all a sorry bunch of civilians."

As we approached Parris Island, the road was lined on both sides with three-story barracks. Heads started popping out of the windows of the barracks. "You'll be sorry," they exclaimed, "You're gonna wish you never came here!" This all made us feel really low. As we moved into the center of the base, we saw a flock of tents. These were pointed out to us as our quarter during basic training. Fortunately, Hookers and I were assigned to the same tent. We were told to find a sack. Each tent held ten men. We were told to drop off our belongings and come right out and line up between the tents. A sharp looking Marine came over to us.

"I'm Sergeant Longo. For the next eight weeks I will try to make Marines out of you. From now on you'll address me and every one of your superiors, regardless of rank, as "Sir." Do you hear me?"

"Yes, sir!" we replied.

"Louder!" he commanded.

"Yes, Sir!"

"Anyone here from military school? OK, no one. Anyone here with marching experience?"

"Yes, sir!" I cried, "I marched in a drum and bugle corp!"

"Well, this is no drum and bugle corp.," he barked.

Sergeant Longo, our Drill Instructor and Corporal Edwards, his assistant, marched us up to the barber shop. As we each took turn in the barber chair, the barber would politely ask, "How do you want your haircut?"

"Oh, just give me a light trim," we'd say.

Zip, zip, zip! All the hair came off, and the barber would howl. It didn't take long for fifty haircuts to be completed. And, wow, we all sure looked different!

Next, we marched over to the quartermaster for our fatigues and shoes. One thing the Corp. did was insist you had a good fit. They didn't want anyone looking sloppy and they didn't want anyone to have blisters on their feet. We were issued underclothing, socks, shaving needs, toothpaste, and a new toothbrush. We were issued each a box which was just large enough to pack all the civilian clothes on our bodies and in our bags. These we addressed to home. We knew we wouldn't be seeing those civilian clothes for a long time.

Sergeant Longo made it clear that we would be doing everything as a group. We'd go to chow together; go to the bathroom together, go to sleep and wake up as a group. There would be no smoking either, unless the smoking lamp was lit.

We were taught how to make our beds, which we called "sacks". Each morning, our quarters were inspected. Our sheets had to be folded properly at the corners, and the top blanket had to be so tight and firm that if the inspector dropped a coin on it would bounce. They also stressed that the use of profanity would not be tolerated.

Now, we were ready to concentrate on the art of marching. Every day we would march, march, march. At first some of us couldn't keep in step. Many were out of shape so we did hundreds of pushups, situps, and laps.

We were issued a Springfield rifle, known to us as our "03 rifle." We learned how to disassemble and assemble our rifle in one minute. This rifle would be our most prized possession. We would eat, drink, and sleep with it the rest of our stay in the Corps. Our rifles were extremely old and many other Marines had trained with them before us. We didn't realize at the time though that having a real rifle and not just a stock to train with, was a privilege. Not all recruits in the service were so well equipped.

Saturday, after breakfast, was laundry time. The laundry facility consisted of large tables with faucets above them. We were given buckets and scrubbing brushes and an area for hanging out our clothes to dry.

Our platoon was part of the 10th Recruit Battalion. Each Drill Instructor had his own platoon of trainees and he wanted his platoon to be the best. We were in competition with one another. Any boot that couldn't or wouldn't cooperate was sent to a group called Section 8, where he was either discharged or given a lesser duty.

Each day training became harder, but we started looking better. Our civilian ways were leaving us and the way of the Marine Corp. started to sink in. Every order seemed to get easier, and we started to feel some pride in ourselves.

Though we were down south, it was still cold at night. Our tents had kerosene heaters in the center attached to exhaust pipes. Unfortunately, ours didn't ever work. We complained about it, but no attempt was ever made to repair it. Our buddies in the next tent would poke fun at us, saying to one another, right before taps, "It's so warm in here. We don't think we need our blankets. How about you guys? Do you need yours?"

We were freezing every night, so Hookers and I made a plan—the next time the platoon went to the movies on the base, we would stay back. This is what we did, and after everyone had gone we sneaked into the next tent and switched heaters. It didn't take very long to accomplish, and we had the heater going and the tent comfortably warm before everyone got back. The boots in the next tent started complaining that they couldn't get their heater started. One of them came over to check out our tent, and accused us of stealing their heater. The next day, after breakfast, we were back in our tents when we heard the command, "Fall out! Front and center!"

The Drill Sergeant asked then in a loud voice, "Will the man responsible for switching heaters please step forward! You men will stand at attention until the guilty party steps out!" Hookers and I stepped forward.

"Well, LaCivita and Huchrowski—our furnace installers. You will keep warm cleaning toilets after drills, but before you do that, you will reinstall your heater where it was."

I could never figure out how the sergeant found out about the switch so quickly. On top of all that, our heater was never fixed.

Chorba was one of the boots from the "warm" tent. He liked nothing better than to stand every evening outside our tent and put on a comedic speech about the day's events. He loved to imitate the sergeants and make comments on the activities required of us. One day the assistant caught him giving one of his "oratories," and told him to have a big speech prepared for the next day. The next morning we were marched to the drill field, and in the center of the field was a wooden box. Sergeant Longo ordered Chorba to stand on the box, and start talking. He was not to stop until ordered to do so. We marched all over the field all morning, and finally at lunch he was told he could quit talking.

Another from of a penalty was named police work. You were handed a bucket and ordered to police the area by picking up all the cigarettes butts around the barracks. One evening our whole platoon was given police work, and in the process Hookers accidentally bumped into a corporal. They both got into an argument, and the corporal called Hookers "a son-of-a-bitch." Hookers challenged him to a duel. When I suggested wrestling, both men agreed, and the match was set for the next evening. What the corporal didn't know was that Hookers had been on the YMCA wrestling team. I was selected to be the referee. The only rules we made were two: no punching; and the match would be considered over with one pin. The surface between the tents where they wrestled was all dirt. With both men on the ground, it was hard to see them with all the dust. After five minutes, Hookers pinned the corporal's shoulders to the ground. All the hooting and hollering created enough commotion to draw a couple of lieutenants, who demanded an immediate explanation. Because I was involved, all three of us were ordered to report to Captain E.P. Howe's office. We stood in front of the captain, and he demanded an explanation. Hookers explained to the corporal that you could call him anything, but never could he stand someone calling his mother a name. "What name did he call her?" asked the corporal.

"Well, sir," explained Hookers, "he called me a son-of-a-bitch."

"I can understand how you feel about your mother, son," said the corporal, "and I wouldn't want anyone calling my mother a name either. You are dismissed, until your drill instructor contacts you both."

The next day, our drill instructor told us to report to the kitchen to "ride the range"—or in other words scrub the kitchen stoves. We did that in short order, knowing that we had won the fight.

Now that our platoon started looking good, we were ready for the rifle range. On our first day out, we were sent into the trenches, and were required to mark the targets for other platoons. The targets slid up and down, and after each shot, we would mark the target with a round marker. This marker would give the rifleman an indication of where he hit, and how far off from the target he was. When he missed completely, we would wave a red flag across the target and holler "Maggie's drawers!" Our old Springfield rifles had been fired so much in previous years that bull's eyes were hard to come by. Every boot was given a score and could possibly qualify as a rifleman.

When our turn was next, we moved up the firing line. I had never fired a rifle before, but I could see from watching others fire that the rifles had a lot of recoil. The targets were about one hundred yards away, and each boot was given fifteen rounds which could be fired from three positions. I fired the first round. "Maggie's drawers," called my marker. I fired a second round and at least hit the target. My score was 250, not good enough to qualify as a rifleman.

One of our last assignments was a thirty-mile hike with full gear. We were in good physical shape, and though it was February, the weather was fine. The sun, though kept getting hotter as we marched along. At ten miles, we were given a rest, but already trucks were brought up to pick up casualties. The hike went well for me, and after the thirty miles of steady walking, and my first taste of rations, I was brought back to the base in the truck not as a casualty, and feeling like a full-fledged Marine.

Our platoon completed its basic training on February 15, 1943. It was a happy day. We had a full drill dress parade with other platoons, and the base's marching band. There was a full inspection with the commanding officers and not only each platoon, but each drill instructor was evaluated. Sergeant Longo and his assistant Corporal Edward were very pleased with our performance. Though they had been very hard on us during boot camp, I wanted them to be proud of us. Their hardness instilled in us the ability to maintain discipline under the great Marine tradition. We were trained with the rifle, bayonet, hand grenade, and for hand to hand combat, but our greatest training was this discipline.

The time had come to reassign each boot to a particular area. Since I had been an apprentice on the Pennsylvania Railroad, I scored high in the mechanical area and was told to pack my gear and report to the

Ordinance School and Repair Depot in Quantico, Virginia. I was pleased to find out that Hookers was also to report to the Quantico print shop. We said goodby to our buddies in the platoon: one was assigned to the Paymaster Department, another who scored a perfect score on the rifle range, was to become a mine sweeper designated to fire at floating mines; and the rest, assigned to infantry outfits.

Hooker and I reported to Quantico headquarters, home of the Marine Officers' Training School, a specialized school for the FBI, and the Corps. Development and Educational Command. We moved into a great barracks and had the freedom now to do as we pleased on base after five o'clock. That night we walked around the base and stopped at the USO Club. What a feeling to be able to salute officers and get a salute back! I felt important. We had our choice of food and ate with dishes instead of mess gear.

That first night Hookers and I started to wonder why so many women kept walking around one particular barrack. Later we found out that Tyrone Power was stationed there while going through Officer's Training School. When we figured we probably wouldn't get lucky enough to meet him, we took off for a bar. It was loaded with Marines. The evening was going well until two women, fighting over a Marine, got into a hair pulling contest. The Marines in the bar, with all their training in combat, couldn't get the women to let go of each other's hair. Finally, the bartender stepped in, dumped a bucket of ice water on them, and kicked them both out. Hookers and I decided that the next time out, we'd look for a better place to go.

I requested and received a weekend pass for leave intending to surprise my family back home. Naturally, they were thrilled to see me, and even thought I had gained some weight. I even made a date for that evening and took her to the Eagle's Club in town. My, my! When I walked in dressed as a Marine, it was like the king of England was visiting. I was a hero. The beer, food, and drinks came so freely I started to get embarrassed. The band kept playing the Marine Hymn over and over again. I finally thanked them, took my date home, and went home. My mom and dad were still up waiting for me when I got home. We drank coffee and talked and my parents told me how very proud they were of me. The next day, my mother cooked a big Italian dinner before I said goodby and caught a train to Washington, D.C. When the train had a hold over in Cumberland, Maryland, I decided to get off and take a look around. I walked into a room with a bunch of slot machines, put in a couple of bucks, and hit the jackpot—$100 of coins. I cashed them in for paper money, and ran to get the train. I made it but every seat was taken. I kept walking through cars until I came to the last car. I opened the door, walked in, and a man holds me back and says, "You can't come in here. This is a private car." I started to leave, but a redheaded woman stopped me.

"Don't leave," she said, "We have plenty of room." The people were drinking, laughing, and having a good time. I looked over the commotion to the center of the car and saw a young girl sitting alone. She had pushed back the seat to give herself more room and held a little white dog with a sparkling collar. I thought to myself, "How mean. None of these people are associating with her." So I walked over to her and asked if she wanted some company. She was very rude, and told me to leave. I started walking toward the group gathered over at the other end of the car, when the red-haired woman stopped me and said, "You can't associate with her. She's an up-and-coming star. She's Elizabeth Taylor."

I did associate with the group on the train though. They were an entertainment troop headed for a performance in Washington, D.C. They invited me to visit them backstage if I ever had a chance to visit the theater there. Of course, little did I know, I would be far from the theater for the many years ahead of me.

From Washington, D.C., to Quantico, I took a bus and there met a girl from Alexandria, VA, not far from the base. I told her that I would try to get away the next Friday evening. Friday came pretty fast, so I decided to take this girl up on her invitation. Hookers was going to the Officer's Club that night, so I hopped on a bus to Alexandria by myself. She lived only a mile from the bus station. I easily found the house and knocked on the door. Sure enough, there she was, home alone. We sat on the living room couch and talked for about a half an hour. Then there was a knock on the door. She opened the door, and an Army guy walked in. She informed him that she had other plans for the evening, and that she couldn't go out with him. He looked at me, and I stared back at him and said, "You heard her."

"I'm leaving," he replied, "But I'll be back."

Fifteen minutes later, we hear another knock on the door. This time, before opening the door, she turns the porch light on and moves the drapes to peek out. "Oh, my!" she cries, "He's back with three of his buddies. Quick, go out the back door."

I decided I was not going to fight with four soldiers, so out I went. I heard them holler, "There he is!"

Luckily, I had a head start, because I ran with them behind me the full mile to the bus station. Thank God there just happened to be two Marines at the bus station, who were waiting for a bus to Quantico. I ran over to them, huffing and puffing. The four Army men chasing me rushed in, glanced over to me and the Marines, and left in a hurry! I learned one thing from this experience—never go out on liberty alone in a strange city.

My next two weeks of training were with the 90mm antiaircraft gun. The gun was new, replacing a three inch antiaircraft gun which was still being used in the Pacific. This 90mm was not only bigger and better, but could be directed by radar. My training was to learn the nomenclature of the weapon and its mechanical operation. Still, some Marines didn't think being in Ordinance was macho enough, so they purposely flunked out of school. The class kept getting smaller and smaller. In my four weeks in Quantico I managed to do very well on my tests and even got to see Kate Smith sing "God Bless America" at the base theater, but by then out came a rumor that the next group in our class to flunk would get to go to Hastings, Nebraska, to train as horseback Marines. These Marines would get to guard an important defense plant. Oh, boy! How I would love to be a horse Marine! For the balance of that week, all I could think about was going to Nebraska. I purposely didn't pass that week's test. Major R.G. Dremaond called me into his office a few days later. I snapped at attention. "LaCivita reporting, sir."

"So you want to be a horse Marine, LaCivita?" he asked me.

"I'd like to, sir," I replied.

"Well," he asked, "I'd like to know how you went from the top to the bottom of the class in one week?"

"Being a horse Marine looks pretty exciting to me, sir," I answered.

"Well, you're on the list, but we're only sending twelve men, and you are supernumery."

I understood this to mean that if someone didn't show up, I would fill his place. I couldn't just let this pass me by, so Hookers and I got our heads together again and came up with a plan. We would try to take someone on the list out for a "celebration", and get him so loaded he would sleep in the next morning. Try as we did, though, not one of those guys would "celebrate." Even so, I had all my gear packed, and waited outside the barracks ready to go. Sure enough, all potential horse Marines were accounted for, and I was left standing outside with all my gear. A corporal told me that the Major wanted to see me immediately.

"So much for the horse Marines, LaCivita, and I'm sorry to tell you I can't take you back into the program you were training for now that you flunked that test. You will be transferred to Camp Lejeune in New River, North Carolina. You are to report to Major Hochsmith with "A" Battery, Artillery Battalion Training." So I left Quantico on April 10, 1943. I had my sea bag packed with all my belongings.

When I arrived at Camp Lejeune I was surprised not to see many Marines around., But day by day they came in from Parris Island, Midway, and different units. I felt that these men who filtered in would be the men whom I would spend the duration of the war with. The first real buddy I met was Bill Lawrence from Rhode Island. I, also, bunked closed to two fellows, Clarence Kern and William Feuller, from the Pittsburgh area. We would be trained in special weapons with the 50 caliber machine guns. This weapon would be used against enemy forces such as landing craft and low-flying aircraft. Our target was a sleeve, towed by a plane. The sleeve was attached by a long cable, making sure that the plane was safe from fire. We formed platoons and were assigned to them in alphabetical order. A roll call read like this: "Buscaglia, Butova, Davis, Fueller, Hayden Hedgepatch, Kern, Koczaja, LaCivita, Lawrence, Peters, Reinhart." We were told to acknowledge our name with a "here." It seemed simple, except that the sergeant couldn't pronounce our names. He'd get to Koczaja and say, "Ko-Ko-Ko..." Koczaja would answer "here." Because my name followed his and the sergeant couldn't pronounce my name either I would just shout "Here" before he even started to try. We were "Ko-Ko-Ko- Here-Here" until the sergeant learned our names. Small things like this only seemed to make us grow closer together. We knew we'd be experiencing things together that would make us close for a lifetime. I especially felt something for Bill Lawrence and we started to "pal around" like brothers. Little did I know then that we would soon literally tie ourselves together one day in order just to survive.

chapter

3 From a Train Window

Preparing for combat was our priority now. I completed the 50 caliber gunners' course with a score of 85% and the 20mm antiaircraft test with a 95%. In each class different types of planes were projected onto a big screen. We were to know in an instant the type of airplane, American or Japanese. In 1943 we didn't have a large selection of fighter or bomber planes, and the Japanese air force was built up with zeroes. Besides our antiaircraft weapons training, we were drilled on new ground fighting techniques. Since the Marines were just experiencing ground fighting at Guadalcanal, they were learning fast that new ground fighting techniques were needed for survival. This was mainly jungle terrain, and the Marines learned first hand that the Japanese were violating every previous fighting convention. It was imperative that we be exposed to this new type of adversity. We were determined to be fully prepared to fight such an innovative enemy. At times, the drills were tedious, but we understood that they would pay off. We believed that our performance on the battlefield would reveal our hard training, so our morale was always high. We had pride in being Marines.

Colonel Bittle revised the whole idea of hand-to-hand fighting. During the previous war, the bayonet was about twenty inches long. Men were taught to perry left, perry right, and thrust! Now this system was outdated. The Colonel devised a new system which to this day is called the "Bittle System." First, he shortened the bayonet to the point that it looked like a hunting knife. It was to be kept very sharp. The old system used a stabbing motion, but the new Brittle System used a slashing motion from side to side. The bayonet was made to attach to an M Rifle. Bittle also incorporated into his system "jujitsu" in which an opponent's strength and weight are used against him. The Colonel was amazing. He would have you try to stab him with your bayonet, but with just a shuffle of his feet all you could do was miss him. This training, coupled with maneuvers, completed our training at Camp Lejeune. I had arrived from Quantico, VA, on April 11, 1943, and now it was June.

During this stay Marines were being killed in combat overseas and being shipped home. We were assigned to attend several military funerals. One morning thirty of us were loaded onto a bus in our dress uniform. After several hours we found ourselves at a farmhouse—the only building visible for miles. A large tent had been set up by the house and as we marched into the tent we saw the casket resting in the center. Along side the casket sat a man and women—the mother and father of the killed Marine. Our "chappie" delivered the service and the honor guard fired a twenty-one-gun salute. Then, a lieutenant and three noncommissioned officers removed the draped flag from the casket, and handed it to the mother. Our bugler blew taps, and we boarded the bus. It sure was a sad night, seeing the mom and dad stand near the casket as we pulled away. It was silent all the way home.

The next day, Lawrence, Hayden, Hedgepatch, and I decided to catch a bus on Route 258 and just travel around. We were traveling north toward Kingston. We started talking to a girl heading home and she invited all of us to a square dance at the Kingston's Fireman's Club that evening. She said there was usually a shortage of men at the dances, and that we'd be very welcome. When we got off the bus, she invited us all to her house for dinner. She and her mother were the only ones at home since her brother was away in the Marine Corp. The more we hesitated, the more she insisted. "Ah, ok," we said, "but don't cook anything fancy just for us. "We sat in their living room just listening to records while they prepared dinner. When she invited us into their dining room, we couldn't believe our eyes! The table was set with their finest china and silverware! I felt kind of funny. Here we had just met this girl, and now we were in her house about to eat her rationed food. We all sat around the dining room table. They served us meat, potatoes, peas, and corn, which we enjoyed with lemonade. They were the nicest people! Before we left the house for the dance, we pitched in and insisted they take some money. Later that evening we walked to the dance hall. When we walked in, the band was playing a country and western song, but for the rest of the evening they just kept playing the Marine Corps hymn, too. We had a good time trying to square dance. None of us knew how, but they never tired trying to teach us. We stayed until the dance was over, but by that time there were no more buses running until morning. We were stuck, and we had to be back on base for morning roll call.

While we were standing near the bus station, the local sheriff stopped to talk to us. We told him about our situation. He was nice enough to offer us a ride back to the base and the only thing he wanted was enough gasoline, which was being rationed. When we got the local gasoline station, the attendant saw four Marines and a sheriff. There was no problem. The owner filled his tank, and we got back on base during the wee hours of the morning.

Our time for maneuvers had come, so we packed all the gear needed for the operation. A number of platoons were assigned as the defensive unit, and a number assigned to the offensive. Our platoon was part of the defense group. After the offensive unit left us, we were briefed, and shown maps of the area we would be defending. We were told to look out for rattlesnakes, and to keep our leggings on at all times. We were given a password, and while we were on guard duty, anyone who didn't say it was not to pass beyond that point. We would be defending a certain perimeter, and we didn't know when their attack would take place. We were told to dig foxholes for the night. There was a latrine set up which was built like a baseball dugout covered with a top of dried leaves. Picture a dugout with the ball players sitting in it, except each player has a hole under his seat. Jake Hedgepatch and I pulled down our pants and sat in the seat. "ZZZZZZ"

"Jake!" I said, "Did you hear that?"

"Keep really still, and it won't bother you." He replied. Another minute went by, and again we heard "ZZZZZZ." I jumped up, and out I went with Jake following me. I almost tripped over my pants as I kept holding them up. Hardly anyone used that toilet again.

That evening, we dug our foxholes with little spades. It was like digging a shallow grave.

I didn't feel too comfortable after that, and neither did my buddies. We walked around in the dark most of that night.

The next day I drew guard duty. My post was near a road at the entrance of our holding area. Everything was quiet for an hour, when a jeep comes barreling down the road. When it approached my post, I hollered, "Halt! What's the password?" In the front seat was a major general with a corporal driving.

"I'm the commanding officer. I don't need to give you a password."

Now the password was "little." Most of our passwords had an "L" in them, since the Japanese had a hard time pronouncing this letter.

"I'm sorry," I said. "You can't pass until you give the password."

"I'm telling you," he insisted, "I'm the commanding officer for this maneuver, and I've got to get to the command post."

"Sir," I replied, "You may be, but my orders are not to let anyone pass unless they give me the password." I had no phone, and I couldn't leave the post. Just then, my buddy, Lawrence, came walking down to see what the commotion was about. He suggested that I could ride in the Jeep with the two to the command post. He would take over my duty until I got back. So I got into the back seat of the Jeep, and we drove to the Command Post. Sure enough, he was the Commanding Officer, Major General D.H. Nelson. He explained the incident to Major Hochsmith.

"What's your name, private?" Major Hochsmith asked me. I thought to myself, "Well, here comes some brig time. At least I can't be demoted. I'm only a private."

"Major Hochsmith," said Major Nelson, "I want to commend this private for following orders, and not giving in to me. I'm sure he'll be a good, dependable Marine."

Everyone in our platoon heard about what I had done and thought it took a lot of guts to do it. It seemed like after that day, I always was given a good share of guard duty.

I received my duty classification, which was heavy anti-aircraft gun crewman (90mm) 601. We were the 21st Replacement Battalion. But before shipping out of Camp Lejuene to go overseas, we were given a five-day pass. I headed home, knowing that this would be my last leave for a few years. I traveled back to Pittsburgh with my Pennsylvania buddies, Kern and Fueller. The trains were always filled to capacity with servicemen. We had to sit on our bags for most of the trip, but we didn't mind, because we were going home. We had our dress greens on, and we were proud to be Marines.

My mom cried when she saw me, but my dad always kept his emotions to himself. For the first two days of my visit, we got lots of company. I was happy to be with my sisters and younger brothers. My brother, Lou, had been drafted into the Army, and was in boot camp. The next three evenings, I dated. I wore my dress blues, which made me a sharp looking Marine. Everywhere I went, I was embarrassed by too much respect. I hadn't been overseas yet, but people treated me like a hero. Though I was having a great time at home, as the time for me to leave approached, I could see my mom and dad with that unhappy look on their faces.

My return trip was with the B&O Railroad, which ran through McKeesport, PA, about five miles from my home. I said my goodbyes, and kissed my mother, but I didn't see my father anywhere. It just so happened that our community had scheduled a civilian air raid drill, and everything had to be stopped. As my neighbor was driving me to the station, we were stopped by an officer. I told him I was running late, and had a train to catch, so he escorted me to the station. I bought my ticket to Washington, D.C. and from there I would transfer to a train going to Jacksonville, N.C. I ran to board that train and grabbed a seat by the window. By golly, I looked out and saw my dad standing near a pole in the station. He was crying. He must have watched me at the station. I never could figure out how he got there so fast. That's my picture of a father who never could say, "I love you," but whose actions spoke louder than words. I cried for the next few miles.

When I got back to base, everyone seemed happy. Some men were playing cards, and some were horsing around. Some were engaged in the throwing of shaving lotion on one another. I don't want to embarrass this Marine by naming him. I was sitting on my bunk, reading, and he threw shaving lotion on me. I said "OK, I'll horse around with you!", and when I took his bottle of shaving lotion and dumped it on his prized hair, he started swinging. I grabbed him and threw him over his bunk. He picked up a bayonet at the foot of the bunk bed, and came after me, swinging it. I circled him, grabbed the bayonet, and disarmed him, but the thing that worried me was that he said that he was going to kill me while I was asleep. How was I going to cope with this nut?

We all went to chow, and my buddies told me to be careful. This kid had had a bad life at home. I was worried, but as soon as I got back from chow, a sergeant came in and told this sorehead to pack his gear and report to Major Nelson. I never saw this Marine again. Evidently, someone reported the incident, and he must have been transferred to another outfit.

The next day, we packed all our gear, and boarded the troop train. It didn't look like a troop train. The Marine Corps did it up right! Our pullman cars had sleepers that would accommodate one man in the upper bunk, and two men in the lower. Also, we had our own dining car. We pulled out of Jacksonville, NC, on June 15, and headed north for our train trip across the country. We were traveling to St. Louis. I love train travel. While you are in your compartment at night, there is nothing like falling asleep to the sound of train wheels going clickety-clack. The popular song was "Chattanooga Choo Choo", which seemed to fit the times.

Marines seemed to travel first class, but the Army troop trains were converted boxcars which became bedrooms for attached soldiers. Army baggage cars were turned into mobile kitchens which were manned by their own cooks—but not our dining cars, which were manned by the regular railroad chefs. The lucky few had pullman cars, but most soldiers were transported by passenger cars with four to a seat. They had to sleep in a sitting position. We lined up by car for chow. The car closest to the dining car would eat first, and we moved down the line. The line moved fast, and was very orderly. The food was excellent for breakfast, lunch, and dinner.

I liked to get up early in the morning, before the rest of the pack. Many of the boys played cards, but I enjoyed sitting during the day, and looking out the window. People would wave, and I would wave back. At night, when we were stopped at the station, I watched the workmen on the platform, with their carts loaded with ice. They were servicing our water coolers. There was a lot of hustle and station noise from all the activity. The dining car was being reloaded, and the cars' wheels were being inspected. You could hear the steam engines huffing and puffing. After we were hooked onto another engine, we started moving again. We rode through Kansas and Colorado to Salt Lake City, Utah. Here we had a long delay. We all got off the train, and marched to a cafeteria for dinner. Our commanding officer had called ahead and reserved it. It was a change of pace which we enjoyed. The townspeople at first thought they were being invaded, but they still were very nice to us. We boarded the train again, and traveled through Utah and Nevada. By this time, we were confused. We didn't have any idea where we were going until June 21, 1943, when we pulled into Camp Elliott, CA. We joined the 4th Marine Depot Co. FMF 1st MAC, under Captain Edward C. Apperson. California is supposed to be warm—well maybe during the day. But we were housed in tents, and on the first night I was so cold that I shivered in my cot. The blanket didn't warm me up, so I took all the covers and the mattress off the cot and covered myself with them. We spent the next four days at Camp Elliott. The second night, Bill Lawrence and I decided to go into town. We heard that there was always a big dance at the U.S.O. Canteen. When we found it—man, was it jumping, and loaded with Marines. Bill and I were lucky to get a table. We sat, and ordered a couple of beers. Beer was all they were allowed to serve. The beer had a sort of weak taste. A couple of girls came over, and asked if they could join us. Of course, we felt proud that we had women sitting at our table. We talked, laughed, drank, and danced, and had a good time. The band was playing, and Betty Hutton was singing "Don't Sit Under the Apple Tree." There was lots of smoke in the air.

Bill and I excused ourselves to go to the men's room, and when we got back to the table, the girls were sitting with two other Marines, and wouldn't come near us. The Marine sitting next to our table told us what had happened. The two Marines who took our girls told them that we had just arrived back from the Pacific and while we were over there, we had contracted a contagious jungle disease, so they shouldn't associate with us. They thought this was funny, but we had the last laugh. The next day we found out that the girls invited them to their hotel room, spiked their drinks, and "rolled" them (took all their money). That evening, Bill and I had a few too many beers.

We couldn't walk straight. We were leaning on one another, trying to get through the gate. The guard helped us through, and we were told later that we were seen crawling to our tent. That was my last bash in the states.

chapter

4 The M. V. Bloemfontein

On July 1, 1943, we were transported to the San Diego Naval Yards. In the Pacific, the first Marine action had been August 7, 1942 by the 1st Marine Division in Guadalcanal. The fighting had been ferocious, and three thousand Americans died. Full control wasn't achieved until February 9, 1943. There were still many areas of the Solomons which were controlled by the Japanese.

Most of the Marine operations were under Alexander Van der Grift, Colonel Evens Carlson, Commander Thomas Halcomb, and the great Admiral Nimitz. This was one of the turning points of the war. We were now on the offensive, but there was still a lot of war ahead of us.

At the Naval Yards, we had a great lunch in the cafeteria. After lunch, we lined up with our platoons and marched to the dock area. Our sea bags had been transported ahead of us. They were marked with name tags for identification. They were very important to us. I imagined myself gong on a two-year trip. How big would my suitcase be? How about a trunk? Well, we carried all of our belongings with us—shoes, socks, underwear, clothing, dress uniforms, everyday fatigues, toiletries, blankets, and anything personal that we could fit into the one sea bag. As we picked up our bags, we formed a single line. Just as we got on the gang plank, a girl handed us a ditty bag, and said, "God speed".

My first impressions of the ship were how big, how old, and how ugly it was. It sure could have used a coat of paint! We were directed into the hold. The hold of a ship was in the interior, below the deck. Generally, cargo was carried there. As we moved into the hold, we saw nothing but rows and rows of hammocks which were swinging from ropes at both ends. These were about four high! What a mess! There was no ventilation, and there were no port holes. It looked like we were in a big metal drum.

I happened to get a lower hammock. Bill Lawrence was above me, Jake Hedgepath was above him, and our new buddy, Tim Massar, was on the top. He had to step on a stool to get to his hammock. I set all of my gear down. Our gear created quite a mess, but we managed to cope. I opened up the ditty bag that the girl had handed me. In it was a comb, a toothbrush, toothpaste, shaving cream, and a razor. In my bag, there was a post card, on which was written, "Be strong, and of good courage. Be not afraid wither thou be swayed, for the Lord thy God is with thee, whither so thou goest." It was signed, "Good Luck & God Speed—L.C. Stapley & Family—Sandy, Utah".

I asked if anybody else had received a similar card, but it seemed like I was the only one. I felt then that as long as I carried the card in my wallet, God would protect me. I decided then that after I returned from overseas duty, I would write to the Stapley family, and let them know where I had been, and thank them for giving me words of faith.

The hold had a public address system. The first thing we heard was, "We are on our voyage. If anyone falls over board, the ship cannot pick you up. Repeat: if you fall overboard, the ship cannot pick you up. The water fountains will be on for two hours in the morning, and two hours in the afternoon. Fill up your canteens. There will be times to conserve water—then the fountains will be on only once per day. Here this: if by chance, we are hit by a torpedo, the section hit will be sealed off, so as not to flood out all the other compartments." I could just picture myself floating around in the sealed compartment.

We went up on deck. We were on the stern. We stood near the old ugly rail, and watched the tug boats pull our ship out to sea. Then, we had to line up for dinner. It seemed as though our platoon was scheduled to eat last. It took forever for us to get our food. We were given whatever was left, and we didn't get much. The dining room had high tables with no chairs. We ate standing up. The tables had bumpers on both sides, to keep one's mess gear from sliding off. We found out that we were on the Dutch ship, M. V. Bloemfontein, which happened to be out at sea when the Germans occupied Holland. It was once a luxury liner, but it was striped, and made into a troop transport.

Most American ships were equipped with their own water purification systems, but this old ship depended on large water tanks, which had to be filled at ports. For the first couple of days, everyone was so seasick that no one had any appetite, and the chow lines were small. Sleeping in the hold, however, became unbearable. No one was allowed on deck but Bill and I managed to stay on deck. Every time the below deck order was given, we would hide in the life boats. Once they closed all the hatches, and no one was allowed up or down, we could then roam the deck.

By that time, we had an escort—a sub chaser which kept in front of us. We moved very slowly, and they had to zig-zag for the whole trip. On one corner of our ship, there was an elevated wooden platform, which measured approximately six feet by six feet. It was a submarine lookout station. It did not have a railing. Whoever drew that duty had to sit on top and watch out for submarines. If they fell asleep, they could fall off. I always seemed to draw guard duty, but I was always thankful that I didn't draw that particular lookout duty.

One night, Bill and I were leaning on the rail, just watching the waves, and wondering where we were going. Then, all at once, we heard "Eeeeeeee..." splash! We heard, "Help! Help!". We hollered, "Man overboard!", but you knew what the rules were. I heard that poor Marine crying for help in my direction. I told Bill that if he drew that duty, I would tie a rope around his belt and stay below the shed to keep him awake. He said that he would do the same for me.

Each of us was issued a life belt that held a little tube-like canister. When the tube was punctured, the air inside would fill the belt. That would keep one afloat.

As time went by, life became a little tougher on the ship. We tried to take showers. When we turned the water on, saltwater came out. The more soap we used, the stickier we became. I tried washing my hair with saltwater, and then tried to run a comb through it! We never took another shower on that ship.

The chow lines were still long, and we were always last. We were fed two meals per day, but sometimes, when we finally got to the chow line, we were lucky to receive an apple, orange, or whatever was left. We complained, and we were told that the food had to be rationed in order to last for the whole trip. One Dutch crewman had the nerve to ask why we were complaining while his people were back home being starved by the Germans. Towards the end of the trip, there were men looking for food in the garbage pile. Men were even trying to catch fish during the day, asking the cooks to prepare the caught fish for them. I happened to find where the potatoes were stored, so some of us ate raw potatoes.

We could always tell when land wasn't too far away. Seagulls would then follow the ship, eating the garbage that was thrown overboard every morning. When no seagulls were in sight, we knew that we were far from land.

The PX on board was open for an hour every day. If we were lucky enough to get near the booth when it opened, we could buy cheese crackers. What we did was to take turns positioning ourselves in front of the booth an hour before it opened, to make sure that we were waited on.

Going to the toilet was an ordeal. One learned to control one's bowels, because one had to wait for an opening, and then rush. When all the toilets became clogged, the Dutchmen came up with the idea of building outhouse sheds over the railing. They brought up lumber, and built outhouses on both sides of the ship. They were a sight to see! They wouldn't plug up, because everything dropped into the ocean. The way those things looked, I would never sit on them. What if one dropped off? Would they stop and pick you up? Bill and I regulated ourselves to a nighttime bowel movement, as did quite a few others. The Dutchmen had to break out the fire hoses and flush the deck every morning. Our commanding officer on board was Major Stanford Squire, but there wasn't much that he could do to help our situation.

We docked at Christmas Island, close to the equator. The natives were selling coconuts. They were throwing them up to us on ship, and we were throwing money down to their little boats. Each coconut cost us a quarter. They hit the spot after what we had been eating. We thought how great it was to buy coconuts. Little did we know that coconuts would be with us continually throughout the Pacific. During the evening while we were docked, three girls came aboard, and did the hula-hula dance for us. We threw quarters to pay for the entertainment.

The next morning, we sailed back out to sea. We thought that the ship had at least re-stocked the food and filled the fresh water tanks. But, they hadn't even picked up rainwater, nor the food. Well, we knew we would be eating crackers and raw potatoes for the rest of the way, to wherever we were going.

One night, while Bill and I were on deck, we heard another splash, but no "Help!", and we wondered if another Marine had left us. We must have been getting into enemy waters, because we picked up another escort.

We called this ship a "tin can". It was like a small battleship—small and fast, with lots of firepower. It looked like the type of ship that I would have liked to be on if I had been in the Navy. The Bloemfontein though was armed at the bow with a three-inch anti-aircraft gun, which was manned by our sailors. I believe that there also might have been a 50 caliber machine gun.

During the day, most of the Marines sat around. Some played cards, but big gamblers stayed below the deck in that dark gloomy hold, like rats in a sewer. I heard when we docked that one person ended up with all the money. It was rumored that he sent home over three thousand dollars. He must have been a card shark.

One day, we decided to play "King of the Hill". On deck, there was an elevated cargo hatch, which was an opening with a portable cover. It was flat, and measured about twenty feet by twenty feet. It was excellent for this game. The hatch top was crowded with Marines, and once one was pushed off the hatch, he couldn't get back on again. This game went on for quite a while. It got down to fewer and fewer men on the hatch, and it was getting harder to push the men off. It came down to Tim Massar and me. We wrestled on the middle of the hatch. I got Massar down, and he tried to push me off of him with his foot. One of the button hooks on his shoe caught the corner of my mouth, and split it, and blood rushed out.

I was taken to sick bay. As I entered, there were about ten medical Corpsmen in what looked like an operating room. The doctor looked at me while rubbing his hands together, and said, "Just what we were studying. Facial wounds. Were you stabbed?" "No," I said. I told him how it happened, and had to sign a form to that effect. They told me to lie on the table, and they all gathered around me. The doctor showed them how the veins ran from the corner of my mouth, and where to make the injection to deaden the feeling in the area, so they could stitch the wound.

"Who wants to give the injection?" he asked. "I will", said one young looking sailor. He inserted the needle, but he hadn't tightened the needle to the rest of the syringe, and all the novocain ran down my mouth.

"Wait a minute", I said, "I don't mind your lesson but I don't want my mouth to be distorted. Doc, you do the stitching." He did the job, and told me that a wound around the mouth heals quickly, and that he wanted me back in a couple of days, so he could remove the stitches.

The doc was right. It didn't take long to heal. He told me to eat soft food for a few days. I said, "No fear of that. I don't believe that this ship has any soft food."

We were getting ready to cross the equator. We were told by Major Squire that we would be initiated after we crossed it. I learned that if you've never crossed the equator by ship, you were a "polly wog." After crossing, you become a qualified "shellback", and a member of that fraternity. We would be "accepted" by the Roman god of the sea, Neptune. We were all waiting for the big day. Those who were already shellbacks would be in charge of the initiations. That day finally came. The person playing Neptune was wearing shorts, and was holding a large cane that looked like a candy cane. There were some 55 gallon drums, filled with what looked like oil. Since oil floats to the top, the drums were actually filled with saltwater, but we weren't sure of that. There were also some cans of lard.

The shellbacks gave the orders. If you were told to jump in one of the drums, that's what you did. Some were plastering lard on men's heads. Neptune had a paddle to give swats to the lucky ones who were not told to jump in the drums, and who were not plastered with grease. Some men were made to act and sing like the Andrews Sisters. Some were given grass skirts, and did the hula-hula. At least the day broke up the boredom on this ship. This crossing of the equator must have been a big deal, because in my records I received a verification certificate stating "Impervium*Neptuni*Regis", signed by E.C. Ipperson, Captain, U.S.M.C.R.

We still didn't know where our final destination would be. Once a day though, someone gave us the latest "scuttlebutt". We heard Australia, and then New Zealand. Some heard that we were going to Guadalcanal. The truth was that no one on the ship, not even the pilot, knew. The ship traveled under sealed orders. At certain points during the voyage, sealed envelopes were opened, giving directions for the next part of the journey. This happened throughout the whole voyage.

At this point, we were having boxing matches on board the ship. The top of the center hatch made a perfect ring, except that there weren't any ropes. They held five or six matches per day, depending on the number of volunteers.

The deck was always loaded. Even the booms had Marines sitting on them, hooting and hollering. They would cheer for the Marines from their platoons. Big Tom Massar was matched up one day. The prize was two packs of cigarettes for the winner, and one pack for the loser. Most everyone smoked, and our supply was getting low.

These matches lasted for three rounds. Massar was giving his opponent a beating. Our platoon had won a couple of previous fights. I was sitting on the second hatch away from where the boxing was. Captain Ipperson came over and said, "You look like a good strong Marine. Why don't we match you up?" All of my buddies were hollering, "Yeah, LaCivita! Get up and box! We need the cigarettes!"

"How much do you weigh?", the Captain asked. When I left San Diego, I weighed 185 pounds, but I couldn't say how much I had lost after fifteen days on the ship with very little food. "You'll do OK," he said. On the way to the ring, I heard an address over the loudspeaker for a person named Taylor to come to the ring. On one end, there were chairs which were lower than the ring. There were two rows of nurses sitting in them. They were going for duty on a hospital ship in the Pacific.

The attendant in my corner was a big Marine captain. Then came Taylor. He been assigned to the ship's gun crew. The ship's crew had their own quarters with decent facilities, which included a gym to help them keep in shape. Taylor looked good. He was wearing a pair of boxing trunks. I was out of shape, and wearing a pair of long fatigues.

The Captain told me, "Watch out. This guy is the state boxing champion of one of the northwestern states. So far, he has knocked out everyone he's fought on this trip."

"Yeah, thanks a lot," I thought. "Now you tell me."

My buddies were making remarks, "LaCivita, what time do you want us to wake you up? Have a good sleep!"

What they didn't know was that I had boxed for the Wilmerding YMCA boxing team, and that I had some experience. The only thing was that I wasn't in shape. Getting in shape for boxing requires a specialized exercise routine. Sitting around, not even getting the proper nutrition didn't help matters much.

We went to the center of the ring. I let go with lefts and rights, and didn't let him do anything. I hit him so hard, he flew off the hatch, and landed among the nurses. I could hear the crowd rooting me on. He got back on, and he still hadn't touched me. I knew that I had shaken him up a bit. The round ended, and the Captain wiped me off with a towel. He said to ease up a bit, and reserve my strength.

We went to the center of the ring, and I kept punching. Again, I hit him while he was backing up, and I knocked him off the other side of the hatch.

By this point, I was getting tired. I started to ease up. He got in a few good punches, but I had knocked some of his strategy out of him. His punches weren't doing much damage. During the third round, we exchanged punches, but by the last half of the round, my arms were sore, and my legs felt like rubber. Since he was in good shape, he started to get the best of me.

The round ended, and everyone kept yelling, "Another round! Another round!" The referee came over and asked me if I would go for another round. My legs were so tired that they were shaking, and I knew that I couldn't go one, so I refused. The captain said, "You made the right decision." Both Taylor and I got two packs of cigarettes. It took about a half hour just for my legs to get back to normal. My buddies said that I had made our platoon proud. But I knew that if I had been in shape, I could have knocked Taylor out.

The next day, we had to line up for our shots. Even though we had received shots at Camp Lejeune, we had to receive one in each arm. I recall from previous immunizations that some of the tough Marines passed out when they were given shots. The captain who had initiated my boxing match gave me my shot, and said, "LaCivita, I know that needles don't bother a tough Marine like you." We discussed future boxing matches, and how one never knew when you could be matched with a professional, and really get whipped.

We had been on this ship for twenty-four days, and we still did not know where we were going. Then, on the twenty-fifth day, in the early morning, we could see a speck of land in the distance. As the day went by, the speck of land kept getting bigger and bigger. Everyone was excited that we were finally going to get off that big tub after twenty-five days. We were told that we would disembark at Noumea, New Caledonia. I don't believe that any of us had ever heard of it.

My first impressions of that place made me feel just as if I were watching a movie, looking at a beautiful Pacific Island. I couldn't believe that I was actually there. There were military trucks waiting to transport us into the unknown. We were told to pickup our sea bags, and to line up on the dock with those bags in front of us. We waited while some of the sailors carried sea bags down the ramp and set them on the dock. They set out about eight bags which no one claimed. I wondered if that many could have fallen overboard, or if some Marines were going to stow away. All of the unclaimed bags were tagged, but we never got close enough to know who they belonged to.

"Bloemfontein" (fountain of flowers) was a beautiful name for a ship, but that was the only good thing about it. I hoped that all the other troops who were transported on this ship had a better experience than I did. We just didn't seem to be appreciated by the Dutch sailors. Goodbye, goodbye, you big old ugly floating tub. As we boarded our trucks, I was happy that at least everyone who I knew was accounted for.

chapter

5 War and Games – the Russell Islands

The first thing that impressed me about the people of Noumea was how they could balance themselves on the edge of a porch while excreting waste. Since we were driven to a new part of the island, where the base camp was, I never did have any contact with any of the people. As we got off the trucks, we ordered to line up in a double row, facing each another.

A colonel came down the center of the ranks. As he inspected the Marines, he would choose one and say, "You! Step out!" As he moved between the rows, he stopped in front of me, looked me over, and shouted, "You! Step out!" He picked out about thirty Marines.

The thirty of us moved far into the jungle area on trucks. We finally stopped at a large field with rows of tents. When we got off the trucks, he told us in a tough voice, "You are going to be Marine Raiders."

I thought to myself, "Now all the special training they gave me in the states is going to be put to use." The colonel had just come back from New Georgia, where the 4th Marine Raiders had just about been wiped out. I believed that the 1st Marine Raiders were also in the same area.

Major Apperson told us before leaving that some of us would be back at the transient center. Tim Massar, Jake Hedgepath, Bill Lawrence, Wilber Davis, William Fueller, Frank Peters, Adam Koczaja, Clarence Kern, Joe Hayden, William Reinhardt, and Earl Cole were all pulled out of line, too. The first day, we ran laps with our rifles and backpacks.

We were broken up into squads and I was happy to be in the same squad with Bill Lawrence. We had done some exercise each day on the ship, but not enough to keep in shape, especially considering the lack of good food.

One evening after training, some of us decided to play touch football. As we were playing, Colonel Carlson happened to walk by.

"So you boys like football. Well, my boys, we don't play touch football. We play tackle football."

We had to play tackle football, and the losers had to run laps, so the game really became tough. While I was running after Tim Massar, I stepped into a hole, fell down, and sprained my ankle.

"You're OK", I told myself, don't let a little sprain bother you." I hobbled around, then went to sick bay, where a medical Corpsmen gave me an ankle wrap.

After a week-and-a-half, we were lined up. Once again, all the names were called, and the men were told to step out of line. All the men I mentioned, thirteen of us, were called upon. Colonel Carlson told us to pack our gear, because we would be trucked back to the transient center. We found out that our records had not been sent on time to New Caledonia. They were to come from the headquarters of the 1st Marine Amphibious Corps, Fleet Marine Force in New Zealand. Major Apperson knew that there was no way that we would be in the Raider Battalion after all the time that we had previously spent in training for the heavy anti-aircraft group. We had been Carlson's Raiders for a little over a week, and we felt that that was long enough.

At the transient center, while we were waiting for an assignment, we drew various chores. Some of the Marines were sent out to scatter stones on the dirt roads which were being built. I was sent to the mess hall to work in the kitchen. I helped to peel spuds, and to serve the line.

One morning, the cook told me to make the lemonade. I told him that I would be happy to, so I went outside and picked a bunch of fresh lemons. He asked me, "What are you going to make with those things?"

"You told me to make the lemonade," I replied.

He started to laugh, as if the fellows were really going to have fresh lemonade, and then he blurted, "We don't use those things. See that gallon can on the shelf? Dump it all into that galvanized thirty gallon can, and stir in about a pound of sugar. That's how we make lemonade around here." That sure squashed my thoughts of fresh lemonade.

On August 8, 1943, we embarked from Noumea, New Caledonia, on board a U.S. built liberty ship. The twelve of us that were delayed by Colonel Carlson were the only ones from the Bloemfontein on board, because the others had left ahead of us. The experience of traveling on board this ship was the complete opposite of that of the Bloemfontein. We had all the fresh water we needed for showers. Drinking fountains had cold water all the time, and we ate decent meals in a nice dining hall. The sailors treated us with respect. They even gave us ice cream and fresh milk for breakfast. We now know that we had been assigned to a heavy anti-aircraft gun crew battalion somewhere in the Solomons.

Under Military Specialities, my classification was listed as "heavy anti-aircraft gun crewman (90mm) 601." The 90mm anti-aircraft guns, which replaced the World War I vintage three-inch guns, fired a twenty-three pound projectile, with a maximum range of 39,500 feet. These were part of the defensive battalions.

(The origins of the defensive battalions reached further back into Marine history than did those of most of the other special units of World War II. Marines had traditionally been assigned with the capture and defense of bases which were needed by the Navy in times of war.

On December 8, 1933, the Fleet Marine Force was established as an integral part of the fleet organization. The primary responsibility of this force was the "seizure and temporary defense of advanced bases." By the summer of

1939, the proposed units were known as defensive battalions. They tentatively were to be equipped with:

12 three-inch anti-aircraft guns
48 .50-caliber anti-aircraft machine guns
48 .30-caliber anti-aircraft machine guns
6 searchlights
6 sound locators
6 naval five-inch guns

A single table of equipment and table of organization were never developed for the defensive battalions. Weaponry and personnel assignments reflected the specific requirements of the unit's destination. During the war, defensive battalions included infantry units and tank platoons. However, the combination of machine guns, anti-aircraft guns, and five-inch guns was the most common. The actual formation of defensive battalions started in late 1939, and seven of them were in existence by the time Pearl Harbor was attacked. The 1st, 2nd, 6th, and 7th were formed at the Marine base in San Diego. The 3rd, 4th, and 5th were organized at the Marine base on Parris Island.

The 5th Defensive Battalion, under Colonel Lloyd L. Leech, was deployed to Iceland in June of 1941, as a part of the 1st Marine Brigade. The Brigade also included the 6th Marines, the 2nd Battalion, the 10th Marines, and various supporting units. Army forces were sent in March of 1942 to relieve the Marine Brigade. The 5th Defensive Battalion, along with the remainder of the 1st Marine Brigade (provisional), returned to the U.S. for reassignment.

All but one of the remaining six defensive battalions which had been organized by the time of the attack on Pearl Harbor were deployed in the Pacific theater. That one was the 2nd. As the U.S. fought more and more on the offensive, increasing numbers of Marines arrived in the southern Pacific area, and many found their way into defensive battalions. The Corps continued to form these units after the outbreak of war. In fact, by the end of 1942, their numbers had doubled, to make a total of fourteen. By early 1944, this total had grown to twenty. All but two of these units saw service overseas before the end of the war. C. C. Cheatham, Marine Historical Records.)

We made friends with some of the sailors on board the liberty ship, and they knew that we were headed for the Solomons. On our third day away from New Caledonia, we spotted land. Someone said that it was Guadalcanal. We kept moving closer, and we anchored about three miles out at sea. We were rushed into quickly picking up our gear and sliding down the nets into a higgins boat, which took us in to the shore.

There was a small airstrip which wasn't very well maintained, so it could not have been Henderson Field. There wasn't anyone around to tell us where to go, or what to do. It was early evening, so we decided to set up our sleeping gear somewhere on the beach. We thought how great it was, that we were setting up our sleeping gear next to a high lookout tower which wasn't manned. There we were, twelve of us, with all our gear and no idea what to do. My sprained ankle was killing me. I removed the wrap to find that my whole foot was swollen.

I sat down to re-wrap it, and I heard a truck barreling up the beach towards us. The driver stopped the truck, and started screaming, "Quick! Hurry! Pick up your gear and get on this truck. Let's get the hell out of here!" He drove us into the wooded area about one hundred yards away, and started shouting again, "Get off, and find yourself a foxhole. We heard planes in the sky, and we could tell by the sound of the engines that they were getting closer. As we were trying to decide who would get the one foxhole, all at once the searchlights lit up the sky. One could see the tracers from the .50-caliber machine guns. The 20mm, 40mm, and 90mm guns were booming away. As we were standing there, watching what looked like fireworks, someone said, "It's just like in the movies." Right then, a Japanese zero flew above the treetops. All four of us dove into the foxhole, one on top of the other. I was on top, facing up. What a sight it was, seeing the searchlights on the zero, while the plane almost skimmed the coconut trees.

We knew then why there had been a rush to get us off of the ship. During the air raid, we heard a big explosion, and we saw something burning out at sea. By golly, they had a direct hit on the ship which we had just disembarked from. I had never realized that a ship, with all that metal, could burn so quickly. The ship became red hot and burned for a while, and we watched it go under.

This was our initiation into the Pacific. We asked ourselves: what if they had decided to keep us aboard the ship until the morning? What if we had sailed in an hour later? Did the ship make an out of way voyage for us? We never heard more about the sinking of that ship. The raid took place on about August 12, 1943. We have no records of the ship that transported us to Guadalcanal, or of the LST that took us to the Russell Islands. Maybe they forgot to put those things in our records.

We didn't get any sleep that night. We saw bodies floating onto shore the next morning. We wondered if anybody had survived. For most of the day, no one came around to give the twelve of us any directions. By the afternoon, we were hungry. Then we spotted a Marine guarding a large stack of food up the beach. We approached, and asked him if we could have some. It was covered with a tarp. At first he said no, because the food was being shipped to New Georgia. We started to walk away when the guard said, "I'm going to look for an outhouse. I'll be back in ten minutes." He just as much said, "Help yourself."

We lifted the tarp, grabbed a couple of large long tins which appeared to contain Spam, and grabbed some small round cans which contained pears. We opened up the Spam, and ate big chunks of it. We ate the pears, and we were satisfied.

Later on, a sergeant pulled up in a truck, and said, "Pick up your gear and load up. You're moving out." He drove us to a small dock area. All we saw was an LST, which is a flat-looking type of ship used mostly for hauling cargo. It was loaded with long timbers which were to be used in the Russell Islands where we would also go. We loaded our gear, and the skipper said, "Make yourself comfortable any place on the woodpile." He was also in a hurry to get moving before dark, we could see anti-aircraft fire at a distance. We were pretty safe moving up the channel. We watched a zero and one of our fighters in an aerial dogfight. The tracers were all that we could see. The zero's engine sounded like a washing machine motor.

We lounged for a while, and slept on top of the timber. The next morning, we had breakfast with the small crew inside the ship. We kept moving up the channel at a slow pace, so we decided to swim along the side of the boat. We had a good time until we saw a large fish streaking toward the shore. At the same time there happened to be a small log floating along the shore. The fish, which happened to be a barracuda, hit that log with its mouth open, and flew up in the air. That was the end of our swim.

As we moved farther up the shore, we started to see activity. The LST pulled in and dropped its ramp. We could see that the Seabees were in the process of building a dock. I saw two panel trucks with their back doors open. Inside each truck, there was a shelf-like setup. A small higgins boat approached, sailing close to the shore near a platform. Two men jumped down into the boat where dead bodies were stacked. One man would grab the feet, while the other would pick up the head. They swung each of about a dozen bodies up onto a platform, loaded them into trucks, and left. We were shocked by the way that bodies were handled, but we didn't realize then that those men did nothing but transport dead bodies day in, day out.

The defensive forces around Henderson Field and Koli Point had departed to New Zealand for a much deserved rest. During the New Georgia phase of the Northern Solomons Campaign, various defensive units were utilized. In August, six tanks were detached from their parent unit, and assigned to the Headquarters XIV Corps, U.S. Army, at Rendova. The Tenth Defensive Battalion in the Russell Islands was still in range of hostile Japanese aerial forces.

As we got off the LST, we were greeted by Sergeant Gorden MacDougall, who welcomed us to the Tenth Defensive Battalion. We were driven to headquarters, where we met Major Cyril Emrich, who gave us a warm welcome. He assigned me to D Battery.

Some of us had developed ringworm from eating raw spam. I had ringworm under both arms. We were told to see the medic, who had a small station set up. He looked at us as if he thought it was funny, and said, "I'll kill that ringworm." He took out a long thin wooden rod with cotton on one end, and swabbed us with Mercurochrome.® Boy, did that sting.

I reported to Sergeant Moore, who was the gunnery sergeant of our crew. He introduced me to our gunner, Guy Parsons; our loader, Charles Cabral; and George Tassos and Albert Parent, who matched up the bleeps on the radar screen. Jake Hedgepath, Art Tucholski, Frank Peters, and I were also part of the crew. Our 90mm gun replacement was built about six feet underground, with sand bags on the top edge along the perimeter. On one edge, there was a ladder for access. Around the inner emplacement, there were bins full of live ammunition.

Our living quarters were also mostly underground, with two-foot sections of screen wire around the top edge for light and air. The top was made of canvas. Each shelter held about six Marines. Parsons, Cabral, Tucholski, Tassos, Parent, and I were in the same shelter. Before evening, Sergeant Moore made us go through a few practice runs to make sure that we knew what our assignments were. All of us were trained for any of the positions, but the old crew members kept their previous ones. The newcomers filled in the unmanned positions.

Most of the marines in the 10th Defensive Battalion had been overseas long before Pearl Harbor, Midway, Johnston, Palmyra, and Samoa were being defended by Marine defensive units. With all those veterans still privates, I could see that promotions would be few and far between. That didn't bother me. Just being a Marine was a promotion enough.

Our warning system was a man posted on guard duty, wearing earphones, from which he would get orders from the command post. He would crank the siren, and at the same time, holler either "One beer!", or "One wine!" "One beer" meant that incoming aircraft had been identified with radar as enemies. "One wine" meant that the incoming aircraft had not been identified, and that we should hold our fire until positive identification had been made.

Once, as it was getting dark, and everything was calm, I heard "One beer! One beer!" from the guard post. At last, we would be firing on real planes, but I was nervous. Sergeant Moore had the earphones on. I could hear the airplanes' engines getting louder and louder, but I couldn't see them. Suddenly, the search lights went on, and I heard, "Commence firing!" Boom, boom, boom! All of our 90mm anti-aircraft guns were firing. The planes dropped their bombs, and came in low to strike. Whoom, whoom! Our 40mms and 20mms opened fire. You could see the tracers in the sky. We fired for about ten minutes. The bombs that they dropped did no damage. This type of incident soon became an everyday routine. When our gun crew started to gel as a team, we could average about twenty-two rounds per minute. This was pretty good, considering that each projectile weighed twenty-three pounds, and that the loaded shell, together with the projectile, weighed close to fifty pounds. We continued with such a routine daily for about three months.

Before the war, the Russell Islands had been made up of beautiful coconut tree plantations. The natives maintained all the groves. When the war broke out, though there wasn't much ground fighting in the Russell Island, there was a lot of aerial action. I saw some native men working around the dock area. They had designed tattoos for their bodies, and all their teeth were brown from eating a betta nut. We were warned to not eat the nut, unless we wanted brown teeth. By the time that I was in the Russell Islands, these plantations were in bad shape from lack of maintenance.

Our battery was set up about one hundred yards from the channel. The place was infested with rats and land crabs! There were so many land crabs! They were funny. If you approached one, it would run backwards. They had fat bodies, long legs, and large claws. These land crabs were not edible, and they made a lot of noise as they scurried. During my first night in the shelter, I was awakened by a scratching noise around the screen area. I couldn't figure out who would be scratching our screen, and moving all around our shelter. No one was concerned, but I had to see what was making all that noise. I got my flashlight and my rifle, and tiptoed to the noisy area. I shone my light on the land crabs. For some reason, the land crabs loved to run their claws against the screen area. My buddies knew that, and they were used to the noise, but they got a kick out of watching me. At night, when a jeep or truck drove up the road, there were so many land crabs on the road that, as they were run over, you would hear pop, pop, pop! The road would be splattered with them. There were also so many rats on the island, that you had to keep your pant legs inside your boots, or the rats would run up your legs.

One day, I was coming back from the mess hall which was close to the channel. It looked like an outdoor pavilion. It was constructed of logs, and had tables and benches with a nice kitchen setup. As we were walking up to our shelter, all at once, Art Tucholski started jumping around. His pant leg had come out of his boot, and a rat had run all the way up to his groin. I never saw a pair of pants come off so quickly.

Our chief cook was Ervin A. Paschkie. He made some pretty good meals. Of course, we had powdered eggs and potatoes, and canned bacon, but all of his food tasted pretty good to me. When we received a shipment of flour, we had freshly baked bread. For about a week, I ate the thickly cut slices with New Zealand butter. The bread had raisins, but most of the men kept pulling the bread apart into little pieces, and eating it that way. I thought, "Oh well. Maybe they don't like raisins." I asked my buddy, Bill Lawrence, "Don't you like raisins?" "Raisins?! Look closely, Pete." He showed me that there were raisins, but they were mixed in with rat turds. The cook didn't like the men pulling his bread apart, so he mixed raisins in the dough with the turds.

Deciding we wouldn't have any more of that, we sifted the flour out of the one hundred pound sacks, and placed it in empty five gallon covered tin cans, which had been used for powdered foods. It was amazing that for every one hundred pound sack of flour that we sifted, we accumulated about two gallons of rat turds.

We built rat traps, and caught hundreds of them. This may sound cruel, but we had to get rid of them, so we created a game. We would take all the rats about thirty yards into the channel, and with sticks, we would see how many we could keep from making it back to shore. It was like a golf game with an animated ball.

In our shelters, there was netting around our cots, because mosquitos were another thing that we had to put up with. When you were on watch, you had to keep a head net on. Art Tucholski, whom we called "Ski", kept a half loaf of bread for a snack. In order to keep the rats from getting into it, he hung it from the center of the netting in his cot. One night we were all asleep, when we heard some commotion. Ski had upset his cot, and was trying to get out. Two rats had eaten a circle around the top of his netting to get at the bread, and they had fallen through on top of him. We kidded him for a long time about that.

At night, if we had to man our guns, we had contests to see who could be the first one dressed and into gun placement. George Tassos could never be beat. He was always first and he had it down to a science. Before he joined us, he had been stationed on a battle wagon. One night, Ski nailed George's shoes to the floor. We were all asleep, when we were awakened by the siren, and "One beer! One beer!" We heard a "ra-boom." Tassos fell to the floor. He was the last one out. We laughed and laughed so much that he didn't speak to us for two weeks. But that ended our contests.

We all drew guard duty from time to time. One night, I had to wake up the next man for duty. He was one of the old timers. His shelter was up a path, and it was located about thirty feet from the guard post. I had my flashlight, and I went in to wake him up. He was sitting in his cot, with his helmet in his lap, and he was stirring and stirring water in that helmet. His face was covered with D ration chocolate. I asked him what he was doing, and he said that he was making ice. One of the fellows in his shelter said that he had been stirring with his bayonet for hours. I left quickly and reported to the command post. They had someone else take his place for duty and the next day, he was gone. We never saw him again.

At first, you couldn't keep any after shaving lotion around. A couple of "rumheads" would drink it. This must have been common in the service, because the Aqua Velva Company finally added an ingredient to the lotion which couldn't be used internally.

Every day, we were given a pill called Atabrine,® which protected us against malaria. This drug caused a yellow discoloration of the skin, and there were many Marines who wouldn't take it. I took mine every day. My skin was yellow, but lo and behold, many of the men who didn't take it contracted malaria. It wasn't a pretty sight to see them shiver and shake. As hot as it was, they would be sweating, and they couldn't keep warm. After they got it, the only thing that they could do was to wait it out. They claim that once you have it, it can come back years later. I was sure that "someone" was watching over me.

One night, we got a "one wine" signal, and we waited and waited, and nothing happened. I was getting sleepy, so I stretched out on some sand bags, and used a big rock for a pillow. All at once, we heard a plane over the trees. It swooped down, and we could see that it was a Japanese plane. We thought that it had sneaked in under our radar. The pilot dropped his bombs harmlessly into the channel. We all jumped into position, and heard, "Hold your fire!" Right behind it was one of our night fighters. The zero tried to get away, but our searchlights were now on it. Our fighter blasted it out of the sky. We had been kept from firing because our fighter was on the zero's tail all along.

Our battery needed a barber, so my good buddy, Bill Lawrence, who was with the radar unit, was handed some clippers and a pair of barber shears, and was told to be the barber. They set up a little shed as a barber shop. I was his first customer. He did OK for the first time, but thank God, my hair grew back. Bill was able to charge 25 cents for a haircut. As time went by, he got better and the clipper wasn't pulling too much hair.

I didn't know that we had a dentist until I broke a tooth in half. It was the one from which I had had the nerve removed back home. The dentist had a tent set up, and his drill was run mechanically. The helper would pump with his feet while the dentist used the drill. He said that my tooth was too far gone, and that he would have to pull it. He gave my gum a shot of novocain, but when he went to pull the tooth, it broke off flush with the gum. He said that he would have to chisel it out. As he held the chisel in place, he told his helper to tap, tap, tap. This went on for about an hour, until he finally chipped every piece out. What an experience!

As time went by, we were getting less and less air activity, so we had more work details. We were also given more leisure time.

The anti-aircraft defensive units, during the periods from August 15 to October 6 of 1943, met one hundred twenty-one separate air attacks, and shot down forty-two Japanese planes.

Since the Bougainville operation was going on, our details were down at the loading dock, loading supplies for the operation. We were regularly sent out to a gasoline storage area, where high octane fuel for our airplanes was stocked in fifty-five gallon drums. We would roll each drum on its edge to the truck. Then two people, one on each end, would lift it up onto the truck, jump on the truck, and load it. I still liked lifting any kind of weights I could find for exercise.

I found a drum that was only half full, but I was the only one who knew it.

"Everyone stand back! I'm going to load this drum onto the truck by myself," I said.

"That'll be the day! We've got to see this!" they cried.

I rolled the drum on its edge over to the truck, set it down on its side, and put a hand on either end. I bent my legs, and gave a fast lift. I grunted, and dumped it onto the bed of the truck. Then, I jumped up, lifted it, and slid it against the other drums. They couldn't believe their eyes, but no one thought of checking the drum. When we got back to the base, everyone knew that I had done something that was almost impossible to do. Even the major commented about it. They wanted me to do it again, but I refused, telling them that I had almost given myself some kind of rupture. I never told anyone that the drum was only half full.

During leisure time back at camp, some of the men would look for "cat eyes" in the channel. They would dive down to the coral growth, look for something similar to a clam, and they would break it open. Not all of the clams had gems shaped like the eye of a cat, but it was fun. It was the same principle as looking for pearls.

The saltwater channel, which didn't have much of a beach, was mostly reefs with lots of coral growth. Our drinking water came from our own distillation unit. For showers, we dug a well inland, away from the ocean. We were able to draw water which had much less salt, and it was good enough for showers.

In November of 1943, there was still fighting in Bougainville. We were pretty secure, so Major Emerich decided that our infantry training needed to be refreshed.

We were organized into platoons and squads. Some of the men in my platoon were Sergeant Farris, Corporal Borowski, Corporal Hayes, Buscaglia, Davis, Hedgepath, Koczaja, Reinhardt, Massar, Lawrence, Rutherford, Ryder, Hayden, and Brandon. Even though we had been having our exercise drills daily, we lacked hiking skills, so we were refreshed with our ground training. Also, we had to be requalified with the rifle. On November 20, on the rifle range, I was given another qualification as a rifleman by Captain R.A.Sanders. Back in boot camp at Parris Island, I was unqualified because of a low score. That had been the first time that I ever fired a rifle. This time, it was an M1.

At that point, we had the feeling that we were going to be moved, and that we would be taking all of our guns to wherever we were going. In early December of 1943, as I was eating lunch in the mess hall, I noticed an LCT, which is much larger that an LCI. It was floating down the channel. As we watched it, a weird feeling came over us. The ship was all shot up, and there was not a person on board. We wondered how that could be. Did anyone survive? Where was the crew? Did they abandon ship? It kept moving down the channel, as if it had a phantom skipper. We watched it sail down the channel until it went out of sight. Yet another wonder of the war!

One thing that we always missed on the islands was an ice cold drink. At times, the temperature would reach 130 F, and the drinking water was always warm. The only time we could get a refreshing drink was early in the morning before the sun came up. I learned to chop the top off of a fresh coconut and drink the liquid, which stayed fairly cool with the husk covering the nut.

We were well into December of 1943, and we would be spending Christmas on the Russell Islands, We set up a palm tree in the mess hall, and decorated it with whatever we could find. We had a good Christmas dinner of a canned ham, mashed potatoes, canned corn, and fresh baked bread-with no raisins. Our cook also baked some pies with canned fruit. One thing that I really enjoyed was the coffee, especially when it was enhanced with canned sheep's milk from New Zealand. Many of us received packages from home, and we all shared. The things that most of us of Italian descent received in our packages were pepperoni and cheese. These were a big hit with everyone. And, of course, all of the Marines also received cookies.

At the end of 1943, our troops controlled the Solomon Islands, except for Bougainville and New Britain. Everyone was trying to find out the latest scuttlebutt. It was funny, how all of the officers weren't even told, but some privates came up with the latest scoop. Of course most of it was far fetched.

On January 18, 1944, we were all assembled for inspection in our platoons. The inspection officer was Lieutenant-Colonel Thompson of the Tenth Defensive Battalion's First Marine Amphibious Corp. After inspection, he gave promotions. One hundred thirty-six of us privates became privates first class, some who were PFCs became corporals, and a few who were corporals became sergeants. The promotion gave us a few extra bucks on our paychecks.

It was great to receive a letter from home at mail call. I always received letters from my sisters, who would give me the latest news of what had happened at home. In one letter my sister informed me of a hair-raising incident regarding our family. During the war, all telegrams were delivered by bicycle. We lived on an L-shaped street with an empty field between the house and the road. In those days, everyone sat on their porches after supper. One day, everyone was watching as the telegram boy rode his bicycle down the street. People were relieved when he passed by their house. My mother and father kept watching as he made the turn and stopped at our house. He got off, walked up to the porch, and asked, "Are you John LaCivita?" My mother ran into the house. The boy handed the telegram to my dad. He braced himself, walked into the house and handed it to my oldest sister, but she wouldn't open it, either. They were afraid of what might be in it. My dad walked back out onto the porch and sat on the swing. My younger sister finally opened up the telegram, and my mother asked, "Who is it? Pete or Louie?" (My brother was in France at the time.) My sister looked up with a big smile, and said, "Neither." My mother ran out to tell my dad that Pete and Louie were OK. The telegram reported the death of a distant relative who lived in New York.

I used to write home at least once a week, but I remember that some men very seldom wrote home. Their parents would complain to the Red Cross, who in turn would notify our commanding officer. He would call the person in, and he would make them write a letter home in front of him.

We finally got the orders to move. There would be no replacements. We were to take all of our weapons with us, except for the Seacoast Navy five-inch guns. Stevedores loaded the ship as we moved the guns and equipment to the dock area. All of our ammunition and weapons were loaded onto the S.S. Santa Cruz. Many of our trucks and jeeps were on the deck of the ship. They were loaded with full five gallon water cans. We embarked aboard the Santa Cruz on February 9, 1944 at Banika Island, of the Russell Islands, of the Solomons, and sailed away on February 10. The ship was really loaded down, but everything was very well organized. Bill Lawrence and I stayed on deck, and never went below, except at chow time. We would lay on the deck at night, and watch the stars.

Washing Clothes -- Boot Camp

Parris Island, S.C.
Boot Camp
1942
10th Recruit BN

Parris Island -- Boot Camp 1942

10th Defense Battalion F.M.F.
Back from the Russell Islands

Bottom: O'Keefe
Top: LaCivita - Lemon

Bottom: Lawrence - LaCivita
Top: Hedgepath, Cole

Hawaii Transient Center

LaCivita

1944

Lawrence

10th Defense Battalion
First Marine Amphibious Corps
Fleet Marine Force Pacific

IMPERIVM NEPTVNI REGIS

TO ALL SAILORS WHEREVER YE MAY BE GREETING

Capt
USMCR

Crossing the Equator
July 1943

Hawaii 1944

Parsons, Peters, Tucholski

Hawaii Transient -- Center 1944

TENTH DEFENSE BATTALION
FIRST MARINE AMPHIBIOUS CORPS
FLEET MARINE FORCE PACIFIC

Eniwetok

Landing Craft Tanks

Frank C. Kwiatkowski

More Dead Japanese -- Eniwetok

Terrain on Eniwetok after the Battle

ENIWETOK
ATOLL
MARSHALL
ISLANDS
1944
10TH DEFENSE
BATTALION

Sgt. Collins (left -- killed on Eniwetok)
& Sgt. Ferris (right)

Cover Behind A Tree

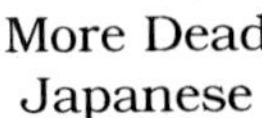

More Dead
Japanese

Japanese Machine Gun At Rest

Souvenir on Eniwetok

Dead Japanese Ready for Burial

Eniwetok Atoll
Marshall Islands
1944
10th Defense Battalion

Angaur - Palau

McKern Sullivan

Hutchison - Sullivan - Johnson - Beatty

Moran

Sign on Bouginville

Johnson

Blanchard - Hoover - Hoyle
Angaur

Hood

Admiring the Beautiful Terrain in the Hills of Angaur

ONE OF OUR
90MM GUN
EMPLACEMENT

1945
ANGAUR

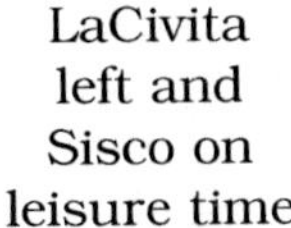

LaCivita
left and
Sisco on
leisure time

Angaur Palau

Thomas J. Massar

Leo J. Sisco

Edward Golanko

Fulgentiz

Rocket Ships
Introduced Latter
Part of War
1945

Rocket Ship
1945

Beach Head
Palau Islands

Disabled Japanese Tank

Credit to the 53rd Seabees

More Caves on Angaur

7th Anti-Aircraft Artillery Battalion F.M.F. -- Pacific

90MM AAA Gun

Angaur
Island

90 MM AAA Gun

90MM AAA Gun
Emplacement
Angaur 1945

Marines on
Angaur

90MM AAA Gun
Emplacement

7th AAA Artillery Battalion F.M.F. -- Pacific

Terrain of Angaur

Shelling Island off Angaur

Out Post
Angaur
Palau Islands
Guarding
Ammunition
Storage

chapter

A Jinx – Eniwetok Atoll

Our ship was not alone. We were part of a whole armada. Our convoy was made up of battle wagons, sub chasers, and aircraft carriers. We weren't going home. That was for sure.

After about five days at sea, we arrived at Tarawa on February 15, 1944. We anchored offshore. We could see where back in November 1943, the Second Marine Division had invaded. During the first four days, there were three thousand purple hearts and about one thousand Marine lives were lost there.

We departed from Tarawa on February 16, and arrived at Kwajalein on February 18. On January 29, Kwajalein had been invaded by the Fourth Marine Division, and the Army Seventh Division. General MacArthur came from the south, and Admiral Nimitz came from the east, moving into the Marshall Islands. An invasion force of forty-one thousand U.S. soldiers and Marines captured Kwajalein after a week-long battle in which three hundred seventy-two Americans, as well as eight thousand Japanese were killed. The U.S. had learned the vital importance of coordinated and sustained pre-invasion bombardment. To avoid another incident like the one at Tarawa, the Seventh Air Force and Carrier Pilots had pounded the Marshalls. We waited offshore in case we were needed, the Fourth Marines and the Army Seventh Division had Kwajalein under control. Eniwetok Atoll would be the next to fall.

We departed from Kwajalein on February 19, and we had no idea where we were going. We did know that our operation was commanded by General Holland Smith, who was under Admiral Nimitz. We lounged around on board the ship. We took our rifles apart, cleaned them, and made sure that they were in working order. Back on the Russells, I had traded in my M1 rifle for an M1 carbine. It weighed less than thirty pounds, and it was a .30 caliber weapon. I liked the feel of it, and it was much easier to handle.

There were always card players and crap shooters who stayed below deck, but none of my buddies played cards or shot dice. If the ship had a set of weights, we would lift and exercise. It seemed that every time we got comfortable on deck, especially in a shaded spot, the sailors would come and hose down the deck with fire hoses. They did that about four times a day. They sure kept the deck clean. The food that was served on board the ship was about as good as could be expected. Of course, I'm not a picky eater. The sleeping quarters weren't bad, but Bill Lawrence and I still played on deck all night.

One day, out from Kwajalein, our officers pulled out large maps, and spread them on deck. They were of Eniwetok Atoll. An officer proceeded to brief us on all of the information obtained from the aerial surveillance of the three islets of Eniwetok. Enjebie was the largest of the three. We all received shots to protect us from the hazards that we would be exposed to. We were told that the flies on the atoll were the largest, meanest flies one could find, and that they carried many diseases. We were encouraged to keep our head nets on as much as possible. We were shown the location of fake artillery weapons on the map. These were set up along the coast to try to deceive the landing forces.

We were told to get a good night's sleep. The next morning, on February 21, 1944, at 0900, the bombardment would start. We were told that we would be going in with the Twenty-second Marines. This would be their first operation in the Pacific. It would also be the first landing operation for my buddies and for me. We were all up early in the morning, and we ate breakfast. Everyone was orderly, and no one horsed around, as we usually did. After breakfast, we were briefed again, and we had an equipment check. We were issued hand grenades, and a supply of D and K rations.

At 0900 on the dot, the first battle wagons opened up with their five-inch guns. We could hear the shells whizzing overhead, and we could see them hit the island. Then, our smaller gun ships, which were close to shore, opened up with all of their guns. While the island was being blasted with artillery, our bombers were dropping bombs. Our fighters would drop bombs, pull up, circle around, and come back to strafe gun positions. Man, what a sight. You would think that no one could survive that kind of pounding.

The Twenty-second Marines were already climbing down the nets on the side of the ship, and boarding the landing craft. As they boarded the boats, the boats kept circling around the ship. The first wave of Marines was moving in for a landing. The battle wagons and gun ships ceased firing. Our fighter planes kept strafing. The Twenty-second Marines were the first wave. We were the next ones to go down the nets and into the landing craft. We circled our ship a few times, and then we headed in. We could see the empty landing craft going back to the ships to pick up more men. I gave the coxswains of the landing craft a lot of credit. They had to keep going from ship to shore, and they were under fire most of the time.

Our coxswain told us to keep our heads down. After circling the ship, the craft kept going up and down on the waves. We all became seasick, and we could hardly wait to get off the thing. We sailed into shore, the ramp came down, and we went onto the beach. We were on Enjebie, the largest of the three islets of the Eniwetok Atoll. Bill Lawrence and I stuck together. The first wave kept going ahead of us, and we were more or less doing the mopping up.

The area was covered with weeds about four feet high, and it was slow moving for us. The Japanese had dug shelters into the ground and that kept us moving slowly. Bill and I were about fifty feet apart, but we were keeping abreast. I heard a few shots, and Bill halted.

"He was aiming at you, Pete."

"Thanks, Bill. I owe you one," I said. We came across a Japanese soldier standing in a foxhole with his rifle aimed into the air. He must have been firing at one of our strafing planes when our planes were strafing with .50 caliber machine guns. A .50 caliber bullet hit the barrel of his rifle and curled it up to the rifle stock. It went through his mouth, and came out the back of his head. After death, he was still holding the rifle.

The Marines ahead of us were leaving a lot of dead Japanese. The warning which we had been given about the flies was appropriated. There were many flies, and they were big and greenish in color. Every time I took a drink of water, I had to wave in front of my mouth to keep the flies out. They kept buzzing around my head. During the day, they made it miserable, but they disappeared at night. All of the dead bodies were removed promptly. They would all be given a proper temporary burial on a little island called Lady Slippers.

Right behind us, on the same day, came the SeaBees. They had bulldozers, and they were clearing the area for a new airstrip. On each bulldozer, there was a Marine "riding shotgun". After seven days, all three islets were seized. Our caterpillar driver was a Marine named Lombard. He did all of the excavation for the gun emplacements, and any other excavation that we needed. As the construction SeaBees cleared the area for the airstrip, hi-lifts were loading coral, which would be used for the airstrip surface, onto trucks. The coral would be soaked with saltwater, and rolled to become smooth and hard. As long as the coral was kept alive with saltwater, it would be kept alive indefinitely. It didn't take long for the airstrip to be constructed. When the airstrip went into operation, two other key positions could be invaded. Attacks could be made on the Caroline Islands, and on the Island of Truk. Liberators from the Seventh Air Force and the Thirteenth Air Force could then deliver two thousand pound bombs. In one month, 1,813 tons of bombs were dropped on the Island of Truk, which became useless.

For the first night, we dug our foxholes and stayed in them. The beach head had been pretty well established. Our 90mm guns were coming ashore, so we had to construct our gun emplacements. We always set up along the shore, but as the war progressed in the Pacific, it slowly became apparent that once an island was secured from the enemy, an attempt to recapture it was very unlikely. The Japanese were too hard pressed defending the islands they already occupied to assume an offensive position. The defensive battalions gradually lost their mission.

Their five-inch guns went unused. These battalions were slowly phased out, starting in April 1944. By July 1, only five out of twenty remained. We were reassigned as an anti-aircraft unit. We acquired more 90mm anti-aircraft guns. The demise of the defensive battalions grew out of the fact that the enemy was incapable of threatening an area effectively once the area had been secured by Marines. Along with our 90mm guns, we also had .30 caliber machine gun nests along the shore. We still had our guard stations, and we routinely drew guard duty.

One day a naval priest came ashore to hold Mass. We set up a makeshift tabernacle in a clearing among the trees. He had a small wooden cross on a makeshift tabernacle. Art Tucholski volunteered as the altar assistant. All the men stood in a half circle and took Communion.

Within a few weeks, the airstrip was buzzing day and night with light bombers, heavy bombers, and lots of fighter planes. We had to fire our guns periodically to make sure that they were in good working order. I was a loader, and Guy Parsons was still the gunner. On our first shot, we had a blowback. During the recoil, flames shot out of the chamber. My eyebrows were singed, and I was blinded for a minute or so. Most of the crew members were temporarily blinded by the flash. We were lucky that none of us was burned.

Every morning, we would bathe in the ocean. Also, we would put all of our dirty clothes in sacks, and tie them along the shore in the evening. The waves beating on the sack all night would make the clothes clean without soap. We had set up large tents for shelter and when the trucks came in with our sea bags, we knew that we were there to stay for awhile.

Our sergeant, Rip Collins, had been overseas for months, and had one more month for his hitch to be over. He kept talking about going home, and he was counting the days. I recall when he and Sergeant Farris were walking up a small grade to our makeshift mess hall. I was walking in the opposite direction with Lawrence and Hedgepath. We passed by a truck, which had stopped. We were about thirty yards away when we heard tat-tat-tat-tat. Sergeant Collins had been shot through the heart, and died instantly. Luckily, Sergeant Farris was missed. It just so happened that the men were delivering one of our .30 caliber machine guns, and they forgot to unload it. As a man on the truck was handing down the gun, he must have accidentally put his finger on the trigger and it went off. It was a very sad day. I was part of the burial party which took his body on a higgins boat to the small islet of Lady Slippers, where all the Marines were temporarily buried.

Early one morning, I was on guard duty, and I could hear an airplane engine at a distance. The engine kept sputtering. It kept coming closer to the island, and it finally became visible. It was one of our fighter planes, and the pilot was trying to make it in for a landing. The engine would shut off, and then start up again. The pilot was in deep trouble. When he finally came near to the airstrip, the engine stopped dead. He crashed right onto the strip, and the whole plane blew up in a big fireball. I could see parts flying everywhere. I saw something land about five feet from me. Lying there on the ground was the skin from the poor pilot's fingers. I could never figure out why he didn't just eject, and ditch the plane near the island.

Some of the men were being used to unload ships. Quite a few items were being shipped to the officer's club on the island. One day, the men were unloading orange juice, and they stole a couple of cases. They were caught, so each day, they were given special work assignments. The funny thing about it was hearing Sergeant Farris on the hill every morning hollering, "Orange juice raiders, front and center!" From then on they were always called the orange juice raiders.

I remember when Bob Hope came to our island for his performance. Before his arrival, a stage was erected by the SeaBees. There were logs placed in the area to serve as seats. The first five rows of logs were reserved for the officers. Before the show started, however, Bob Hope made everyone move out of the theatre area, and said, "When I count to three, everyone find a seat!" I don't think that too many officers made it to the front five rows.

A lesser known theatre troupe came to the island to put on a show for us. During a skit called "Six Volunteers", six men got up on the stage, and little bonnets were placed on their heads. They were each given a baby bottle which looked like it had milk inside it. The object was that the first one to empty his bottle got a kiss. Then came Zeke Davis, all loaded up, walking up to the stage, and hollering, "I can drink more f_____g milk than anybody!" The MPs duty grabbed him, and he was given thirty days in the brig with just bread and water. We thought it was kind of harsh, but as I mentioned before, no four-letter words were to be used. Zeke was a good Marine who just happened to have a little too much of the moonshine that Hayden used to brew for the officers. Zeke never had only bread and water though, because Rutherford and Ryder, our cooks, used to hollow out the center of the bread, and fill it with meat, or eggs, or whatever we had that day, so that Zeke never starved.

We finally got some non-powdered milk. The day it came, I drew mess duty. The milk came frozen in five gallon cans. It didn't take long to thaw, and it sure tasted good. But we really hit the jackpot when we were given some frozen turkeys. On the crates in which they came, it was written that they had been packed in 1918. Someone said that they were kept frozen on barges since the First World War. Our cooks did a good job with those turkeys.

That night, I woke up because my stomach was hurting. I looked around, and everyone was gone. I thought that they had all moved out of the island and left me there. My stomach got worse, so I ran down to the beach. Then, I thought I saw a bunch of mushrooms growing there. All the men were in a crouched position, and moaning. I joined them. The next day, what I now know was Pepto-Bismol® was flown in. I know that we all lost some weight that day.

One day I happened to be on watch with my earphones on, when I saw an LST which was loaded with ammunition. The crew members looked like they were getting ready to unload. Suddenly I heard "pop, pop, pop." Small bore ammunition rounds started flying out of the barge into the air. I saw smoke. I reported this to the command post, and they told me to keep my eye on it. The barge wasn't more than about seventy-five feet away from me. More and more ammo kept popping. It kept getting worse. I started hollering to the men around me, "Run for cover! It's going to blow!" I saw Al Parent with our water truck backing down towards the barge. He was going to use a water hose on it. I yelled, "Get out of there!" More flack was flying , so they moved out. I saw the barge start to move. I found out later that two sailors had volunteered to guide the barge out to sea, and to sink it. They lifted one anchor, but they forgot to raise the other one. This made the barge move out, and then circle back into shore.

In the mean time, I was calling, "CP, CP, permission to abandon my post!" There was no answer. "CP, CP, permission to abandon my post!"

There was still no answer. All at once, there was the biggest explosion that I'd every heard. The blast blew me into our gun emplacement. It got real dark. I still had my senses, but all at once, I saw beautiful colors. They were formed from the sun shining through all the oil in the air, but I thought I was in heaven. Then I started feeling myself, and I still had the earphones on. I started to hear voices. "Pete, are you all right?" "I'm OK, thank God." Then it started to clear up. Everyone started moving around, and I could hear some moaning. Some of the men got hit with shrapnel. I threw my earphones off, and I started to climb out of the gun emplacement. As I looked out, I saw nothing left above the ground. I saw a five hundred pound bomb which had landed unexploded about twenty feet from our gun emplacement. One of the anchor chains from the LST was wrapped around the spot where I had been standing. The LST had been completely blown apart. We found out that the big heavy ramp had flown all the way across the airstrip.

Everyone was telling stories of what happened to them. One said that he was sitting on the toilet, and it blew him through the screen of the stall. Another said that the force blew his shoestrings out of his shoes. The sad part, however, is that those two sailors lost their lives for no good reason. That LST had carried one hundred twenty tons of ammunition, which consisted of eighty tons of bombs, and forty tons of small bore ammo. The two sailors' bodies were never found.

We had to rebuild our mess hall and our shelters. One evening, we picked up Tokyo Rose on our radio. The next evening, she based her whole program on the damage which was done to our island, and she said that the Japanese were going to launch a counterattack to reclaim it. At that time, we were the nearest to their homeland. We waited, but they never came. We never could figure out how she picked up all the information about the incident. She used to play all of our latest hit records, thinking that it would make us homesick, but it had the opposite effect.

June 6, 1944 was D Day in Normandy. In the Pacific, our bombers took off for the Japanese-held islands of Saipan and Tinian. Nine days later, the Second and

Fourth Marine Divisions and the Twenty-seventh Army Division landed on Saipan in the Marianas.

With all this attention now being given to the Marianas area, our carrier-based fighter planes were being serviced on the land base at Eniwetok. They were lined up in the same space-saving method as they would be on a ship, with their wings folded back, sitting right next to one another. There were over one hundred planes lined up from one end of the island to the other end.

One evening, one of our fighter planes, which was scheduled for a nuisance run over one of the Japanese-held islands, took off down the runway. For some unexplained reason, it crashed into one of the planes on the ground. It caught on fire. I could hear the small bore ammunition going "pop, pop, pop." Then, I could hear the explosion as the plane blew apart. The plane next to it caught on fire, and again I heard "pop, pop, pop," and an explosion. This kept coming on down the line. Men were running all over the place. Small bore rounds with tracers were flying all over the island. There was no place to hide. Men from the upper end of the strip were all running along the beach to the lower end of the strip as the planes kept blowing up.

There were three very large fuel tanks, filled with high octane gasoline for use in the aircraft. We didn't know if the tanks had protective tops. With all the red-hot tracers flying around, we were kept in a nerve-racking situation. If those tanks would catch fire, we would all be goners. This was a situation in which one could not fight back.

I ran past one of our machine gun nests, which was built with a protective top. I heard crying, so I stopped and went in. A tough Marine was hugging his .30 caliber machine gun, and he kept repeating, "We're all going to die. Those tanks are going to blow." The explosions kept getting closer, and more tracers were flying into the air. We were all frantic at that point, but we couldn't fight the problem.

Running along the beach, we figured that if the tanks would catch fire, we had only one direction to go. We would have to go into the ocean, and swim out until we would be picked up. This ordeal went on for what seemed like hours. We watched the red-hot tracers flying over the gasoline tanks. God must have made sure that none of them landed into any of those three tanks. The next day, bulldozers pushed one hundred and twelve damaged fighter planes into the ocean at one end of the airstrip. The Navy didn't keep any more planes along our airstrip.

About two weeks later, the Army Air Force had a bunch of bombers lined up the same way. On one of the bombing runs, a bomber lifted about one hundred feet into the air, and crashed into the bombers along the airstrip. Here we go again! "Pop, pop, pop," and a real big boom with a fireball. We were all running around with no safe place to hide. This time, a SeaBee started a bulldozer, drove down the strip, and pushed one of the bombers out of the row. This made a space which stopped the chain reaction. Twelve bombers had caught fire and blown up, but they were all pushed into the ocean. I hoped that the SeaBee, whoever he was, was rewarded with some sort of medal.

The Eniwetok Atoll had been a jinx. We would be glad to leave that place. The two sailors who tried to move that LST before it blew up, and the SeaBee who moved the plane with all the flack flying around were the kind of heroes that one generally doesn't hear about. So was the pilot who was trying to save his fighter plane, and was not even concerned with his life. If only he had known about the one hundred and twelve fighter planes which were pushed into the ocean.

chapter 7
Unforgettable Outpost – Angaur

By September of 1944, we had been serving with the occupation and garrison forces of Eniwetok Atoll since February of that year. We would be leaving soon as our replacement Marines would come in. Then, on September 15, we made a switch. When the Fifty-second Defensive Battalion came ashore, we embarked upon their ship. We left all of our defensive weapons in place for them. We were told that we would be headed for the Hawaiian Island. All of us would be leaving the Tenth Defensive Anti-Aircraft Battalion. Some of the men would be going home, especially those men had been overseas since before Pearl Harbor. Most of us would be transferred to Hawaii.

In the early part of October 1944, we arrived in Kauai, which lies ninety-six miles west-northwest of Honolulu on Oahu. Kauai is the fourth in size, and the most northern of the larger inhabited islands of the Hawaiian group. It is the Garden Island. This used to be a paradise for servicemen. Places like Hanapepe, Kalaheo, Kalva, Kapaa, and Hanalei on the upper end of the island each had a U.S.O. club with great facilities. They even had dances on weekends. At an earlier time, the servicemen from the Army, Navy and Marines, had abused most of the U.S.O. facilities, and had run out of control into the towns. Quite a few of the natives were of oriental descent. This gave them a bad impression of the U.S. Marines, and it was noticeable. Most of the natives stayed at home because they didn't want to socialize with us. Accordingly, most of the Marines stayed on the base.

We were briefed about trying to build up our image with the civilians. While there we helped set up a couple of 90mm anti-aircraft guns, 40mm and 20mm guns, and .50 caliber machine guns along the coast. We trained new Marines almost every day. A long cable with a sleeve attached to a plane would serve as our practice target. Also, we did a lot of drill work, and we kept busy most of the time.

One weekend, five of my friends—Batova, Buscaglia, Lawrence, Hedgepath, and Hayden--and I took a taxi cab into Wailua. There wasn't anything to do. Most of the civilians seemed afraid of Marines. We were told before we left the base that we were to be on our best behavior in order to try to rebuild a good image of the Marine Corps. We had gone for months without seeing any women, let alone being alone with any. But it was next to impossible to even meet any native women. I was sure that they had had their fill of servicemen.

We saw a five-and-dime store, so we strolled around inside it. One of the fellows bought a bottle of cheap perfume, and dumped it on another one of the guys. This started a perfume fight. We kept buying bottles of perfume and chasing around the store. It started to get out of hand, so a girl who was working as the clerk, said, "If you don't leave the store, I'm calling the MPs." We left.

We found a liquor store, and we bought a couple of bottles of rum. "Rum and Coke" was the big drink. We bought Coke, and headed towards the beach. There were some large beachfront houses. We spotted a large empty shed behind one of them and had a drinking party. We were laughing and having a good time until someone spotted a young girl watching us. We told her to get lost, but she must have thought that we were amusing, and she wouldn't leave. She finally said, "You know, you are drinking in the general's dog house, and he will be coming in shortly. We didn't want to find out which general she was talking about, so we beat it out of there pretty quickly.

We walked into town, which didn't have much of a business district. We went into a little country restaurant and bar to get something to eat, and were the only ones in there until three more Marines walked in. During the conversation that we had, an argument broke out about who had the best gun battery. The three Marines told my three buddies to step outside. I talked them out of a brawl, and everyone became good friends. It was the rum talking.

Then we heard of a stable in Kapaa where we could rent horses for a few hours, so we decided to do just that. I had never been on a horse, but I didn't tell my buddies that until we got to the stable, which was located near a pineapple plantation. We all mounted our horses. Mine looked mean. I gave my horse a tap with both feet like I had seen in the movies, and it took off through a pineapple field. A workman in the field started hollering, but I didn't know how to stop the horse. My friends then started to sense that I was not familiar with horses. They kept yelling, "Pull back on the reins!" I finally stopped the horse, but then my buddies decided to race. I was game, so we all lined up abreast. We were racing down a dirt road. I was keeping up, but I was afraid that the horse was going to trip and fall, so I eased up. We rode all over the place, but when I got off the horse, the back of my pants were all wet, and my rear end hurt. The same thing happened to one of my friends. We each had three inch diameter blisters on both cheeks of our rear ends. We couldn't even go to sick bay, because we had been given a warning about horseback riding. Every weekend, too many men were going to sick bay with blisters on their backsides, and they didn't want to see any more. When I got back to base, my shorts were stuck to my rear end. When the air got to the injury, what a smart! My friend had the same experience. We soothed our injuries with Vaseline,® but it was hard to sit for a couple of days. It reminded me of the earlier days in Quantico, when I wanted to be a horse Marine. My buddies called me "Cowboy LaCivita" for a few days.

On November 5, 1944, we had been in Hawaii for about five weeks, and we were being transferred to the island of Oahu. We would move into the Marine Transient Center located above Pearl Harbor. I recall looking into the water as we pulled into Pearl Harbor, and seeing that it was brownish in color from heavy usage. I also observed a very large sand shark as it followed us into the harbor. It stayed with us while the tug boats towed us into port. I reminded Bill Lawrence that this would not be a good time to fall overboard.

We disembarked, and we were loaded onto trucks. As we entered the transient center, all we could see were rows of tents, because this was the area where the Marines were being housed until they were reassigned. It was getting closer to Christmas, and we were wondering if we would be spending the holiday here in Hawaii, or aboard a ship headed for who knows where. But we found that the transient center was a leisurely place to be because all of the islands were overrun by serviceman. In every nook and corner, one saw a uniform.

One evening, our mess hall had been converted into a U.S.O. Club. Everyone sat around looking at one another. The only women in the whole place were working behind the counter, handing out cake, pie, and cookies. Then we heard that Bob Crosby and his band were playing at a place called "the Breakers," and that there would be a mixed crowd. My three buddies and I decided to leave the mess hall and check this new place out. We caught a taxi cab and we rode toward Diamond Head. We saw a large dance pavilion along the seashore. It had a covered roof, with just a fence railing around the sides. The inside was decorated nicely, and sure enough, Bob Crosby was there with his band, playing all the latest hits.

There was a large crowd, composed mainly of servicemen who had been stationed on Oahu. They were all close friends. I noticed that the members of Crosby's band were dressed in Marine uniforms. During the intermission, we because friendly with some of those band members, and we found out that some of them had been assigned to the newly formed Fifth Marine division. They were stationed on the big island of Hawaii. I read in the last letter that I had received from my old hometown buddy, Steve ("Hookers") Huchrowski, that he had finally moved out of Quantico, and that he was with the Fifth Marine Division.

I asked the drummer if he would deliver an uncensored letter to my friend for me, and he said that he would be glad to. He took me to the back room, and gave me a piece of paper and a pen. I wrote about where I had been, and about the experiences I had while I had been overseas. I thought that there might be a possibility for me to be assigned to the Fifth Marine Division, because I heard that they were in for something big. It turned out that they were. They went to Iwo Jima. I found out months later that the letter had been personally delivered to Hookers by Bob Crosby himself.

We spent most of our leisure time lifting weights and playing catch. One time, Clarence Kern, William Fueller, Bill Lawrence, and I decided to go into town for a few beers. We found a lively strip. We saw lots of fights, but we didn't get involved. As we were walking and window shopping, we saw a tattoo shop. We were feeling pretty good, so we decided that we would each get a tattoo. We decided that we would all have the same tattoo – a bulldog with "U.S.M.C." under it – right on our right forearm. We didn't want anything foolish, like some of the men had. Some had dash, dot, dash, dot, with the words "cut here" tattooed around their necks. Some of them had roses with the names of their girlfriends underneath. And of course, afterwards, some of those men received "Dear John" letters.

We couldn't leave the island without paying our respects to the more than two thousand men who lost their lives at Pearl Harbor. Among those men were the one thousand, including many officers, who are entombed in the sunken ship Arizona.

Christmas week came, and we knew that it was not a joyous one back home. All we could do was dream of a white Christmas. This had been the third Christmas away from home for most of us, but I was thankful to still be in one piece. We did receive packages and cards from home.

On January 9, 1945, we embarked upon the U.S.S. Admiral R.E. Coontz (AP122), and we sailed from Pearl Harbor on January 10. I was selected to be a military policeman while I was on ship. There were four jail cells on board the ship, and I was one of the jailers. We had one prisoner, and he was violent. We were never to open up the door to his cell if we were alone.

After a couple of days out at sea, Tim Massar woke me up, and said, "We've got to go on deck. A sailor has gone crazy. He's opening up the hatch doors, and the lights can be seen for miles."

We heard him on the deck, yelling, "The Japs are coming! They are going to bomb us!"

He was making a whistling sound. After a few chases, we grabbed him, took him down below deck, undressed him, and placed him in the cell.

On each cell door, there was a viewing glass which was about three inches in diameter. The second prisoner had not even been in for an hour, when I heard him singing, "I'm dreaming of a white Christmas." He had torn the mattress apart, and he had stuffed the viewing hole, so we opened the door. He was throwing cotton from the mattress pad up in the air while he was singing. He said that he was making snow. We had to take the mattress out of the cell.

Everything went smoothly with the men for the first couple of days, and I had just been relieved of duty at about 12:00 a.m., when the next guard came running up to me crying, "LaCivita, come quick! Number one is trying to break out!"

I strapped on my .45, rushed down to the cell area, and heard a loud banging. I could see the metal door bulging. I looked through the viewing glass, and the prisoner was all curled up in the corner crying, "I want my mother! Mom, Mom, he's going to kill me! I can't breathe! I can't breathe!" He slipped something under the door. It was a ring which he had pulled apart, and completely flattened.

"Please mail this ring to my mother so she can remember me," he sobbed. I really felt his pain. There was no faking or acting from this fellow.

At the bottom of the metal divider, there was an approximately one-inch space between cells. Our sailor, who was small in stature, and wasn't violent, kept heckling the other prisoner. He pretended that he had a tank of gas, and he kept saying, "I'm now releasing the gas. You're going to get sleepy and die." Then he would say, "I'm opening the valve", and he would make a hissing sound. We opened his door, and we told him that if he didn't stop harassing the other prisoner, we were going to put him in handcuffs and tape his mouth.

The violent one quieted down, but he kept asking for water. We got him some water in a cup, and we opened up the door. He was sitting in the corner, all crouched up. I handed the water to him, and he drank it, but he wouldn't give the cup back. We said that we wouldn't give him any more water, and he finally handed the cup back to us. The sailor noticed my .45 revolver in my holster, and said, "Why don't we take over this ship? We can make the pilot turn the ship around and go back to the States." I asked him what state he was from. He told me that he was from Pennsylvania.

"I'm from a town called Duquesne, he said."

"Oh, I'm from East McKeesport. I live about eight miles from you, and I'm going to look you up when I get home. You're probably trying to get a medical discharge, but the only thing you're going to get is some brig time," I replied. He was quiet after that. On January 23, 1945, we arrived at Ulithi in the western Carolines. Both men were transferred to a hospital ship.

While we were docked, a plea for blood donors came over the loudspeaker system. Blood could be donated on the hospital ship, which was anchored not too far from us. Most of the day was spent shuttling men to and from the hospital ship. When the men who hadn't volunteered heard that they would get a shot of brandy after they gave blood, the line picked up.

On February 1, 1945, we disembarked. Then, we embarked upon the USAT Kota Baroe. On February 2, we sailed from Ulithi in the western Carolines. We didn't travel alone. We had sub chasers, and destroyer escorts.

Some of us would sneak up on the deck at night. There was nothing nicer that watching all the stars, just lying on the deck, and looking up at the sky. What a most beautiful sight! The sky was very clear, and we could see the Little Dipper and the Big Dipper. We would talk about home, and argue about who lived in the best state. Since I was from Pittsburgh, they would cough, and act like they were choking. I would tell my Rhode Island friends that Forbes Field was larger that their whole state. I would tell my friends from down south that all they were famous for was Jack Daniel's and moonshine. Of course, any one of us would have loved to be in any one of those places at that time. Then a flying fish landed on our deck. It was the first one that we had ever seen close up. It had winglike fins. We used to watch them during the day, and we tried to judge their distances in the air.

On February 4, 1945, we arrived at the Kossal Passage, in the Palau Group, and disembarked. That same day, we embarked on board LCI No. 460, and sailed from Kossal Passage and arrived at Angaur Island in the Palau Group, and disembarked. We would be joining what had been called the Seventh Defensive Battalion. That battalion was activated on December 16, 1940 in San Diego. It was stationed in Samoa under the command of Lieutenant-Colonel Lester H. Dessez. On March 15, 1941, its arrival gave it the distinction of being the first Fleet Marine Force to operate in the South Pacific. It was redesignated on April 16, 1944 as the Seventh Anti-aircraft Battalion. The islets of Peleliu and Angaur were initially invaded during the latter part of 1944, when they were captured after a month of horrendously bloody fighting that left 6,700 Americans dead or wounded. Eleven thousand Japanese defenders died. Both islets were honeycombed with over five hundred fortified caves and many Japanese still dwelled in caves in the densely wooded areas.

Our officers in the Seventh Anti-Aircraft Battalion were Major Dewey, Captain Williams, Jr., First Lieutenant W.P. Royof, First Lieutenant R.J. Brandenberger, and First Lieutenant Ryan. Our commanding officer was Elmer C. Woods.

Angaur, which is located in the Palau Islands, had many densely wooded areas, but also had many populated areas. The natives had a dark skin with white features and red hair. Others had oriental features. Both the men and the women carried machetes. Word was that the red-headed people were of Spanish origin. The natives were happy to be free again and many were happy to be coaxed out of their caves.

I was again assigned to a 90mm anti-aircraft battery. My gunnery sergeant was Sharpe Kosanke. I liked him a lot. He was a very nice person, and he had been overseas for a very long time. We became good friends. He talked a lot about his home in Salem, Oregon.

At that time, most of us had been overseas for more than two years, and many of the men thought a lot about home. They could hardly wait for packages or mail. It seemed like the longer the time we spent overseas, the more cautious we became. There wasn't much air action, but twice a week, we checked out a different part of the honeycomb caves that had been passed over by the initial invasion forces. There were quite a few Japanese still hiding in the mountainous region. The officer in charge of our battery was Lieutenant Ryan. The Japanese had little railroad cars on tracks which covered much of the area. They also had tanks on tracks. These tanks could disappear into the sides of the hills. Most of them had been destroyed but we used the railroad wheels, which were still mounted on their axles, as weightlifting weights for our morning exercise.

Each night, you could hear the natives singing beautiful songs in the distance. They sure loved to sing in groups. Each morning, all the children were herded down to the beach, where they would bathe themselves with adult supervision. Then, they would sing as they walked up to their little schoolhouse.

Banika Island and most of the Russell Islands were made up of coconut plantations. At the Eniwetok Atoll, in the Marshall Islands, a few palm trunks were left standing among the high brush after the bombing and strafing, but most were leveled by bulldozers to make way for the airstrip. It may have been a beautiful place before the war, but the only beautiful things left now were the beaches.

Angaur, in the Palau Islands, was much larger than the islet in the Eniwetok Atoll, and it seemed to have a variety of trees and bushes. There were many mango trees, which bore yellow-red, somewhat acidic fruit. There were also papaya trees, which bore large oblong, yellow-orange fruit. At that time, this type of fruit was not known or heard of in the States. But small bananas, which grow on a treelike tropical plant, seemed to grow everywhere.

We had a large ammunition dump (meaning stockpile) up in the hills, and we had to relieve the crew for guard duty. Bill Lawrence, Earl Cole, Adam Koczaja, Jake Hedgepath, Charles Branden, and I were all sent up to the ammo outpost. The crew that we relieved told us to keep alert. They had had small groups of Japanese walk in and give themselves up. There the still quite a few Japanese out there. We checked out the great big stockpile of ammunition. We would have to walk through the stacks of crates of grenades, small bore ammunition, and mortar shells. Every so many feet, there was a fire extinguisher. In case of fire we were to use it. Well, after what we saw on Eniwetok, those extinguishers would have to spray a good distance. After checking out all of the extinguishers, we found them to be empty, since the group before us had used them up horsing around.

At night, it was very dark, and very scary to walk through the guard paths. It seemed like I always heard crackling in the bushes. Bill and I decided to sit on top of the stack, back to back, during our four hour watch and all the other men decided to do the same thing.

Our tent was located about thirty feet from the lower part of a narrow road, and we seemed to be like sitting ducks. At night, we posted one man above the tent to guard the three other men while they slept. We had a phone, and we called into the command post every hour.

All of our outposts or guard stations were linked to a communication system, and it would take about five minutes to reach the command post if necessary. At this outpost, we generally got about four hours of sleep at night.

At night, we used to make coffee. We had an old tank turret top buried in the ground, so no flame would be seen. We also became experts on lighting and smoking cigarettes so as not to show any light at night. One problem with making coffee was that it could be smelled miles away while it was brewing. The turret top was located about thirty feet from our tent.

"The coffee is ready, Pete," they'd call.

"OK, I'll get it," I'd reply. But one night when I went and lifted the lid, there was no coffee.

"Hey fellows, guess what? The Japs (sic) stole our coffee!"

That wasn't the only time. So we decided to make two pots of coffee—one for us, and one for them. We knew that the Japanese who were still hiding in the area could have thrown hand grenades into our tent at night. Although we covered the area many times and we could never locate them, we always seemed to find the empty 1 gallon coffee can around our area. On most of the islands, the Japanese forces had mounted suicidal banzai charges, but I believed that the Japanese hiding in the caves around us had a desire to live.

We stored our water in big G.I. cans about ten feet from our tent. At night, they would steal our water, so we decided one evening to tie an empty can to a full one. It was just starting to get dark when I happened to look toward the water cans. I said, "Don't look now. I saw a hand reaching for our water!" At that moment, we heard some rattling. He dragged the cans about five feet, and let go. Our rifles were in our bunk, but we decided not to fire at him.

We had wires with cans tied to them circling our tent. Many times at night, someone would run into them, and we would hear rattling. One time we got a scare when we found an open box of hand grenades in the bushes about thirty feet from our tent. Some were lying on the ground, but we counted them, and none were missing. By not firing at the Japanese, and sort of looking the other way when they needed water, we may have kept them from throwing the grenades.

After a few weeks at the post, we were more at ease, and we got used to the area. One day my buddies wanted to go into headquarters for the day. They would ride in with the jeep that delivered our chow every morning. I said it would be all right if they promised to be back before dark. "Sure, sure, we'll be back," they promised. I had the whole day to myself. Besides the rifle, I had a Colt .45 strapped to my side. There was nothing much to do. I was sitting on my sack, and I spotted a brilliantly colored tail sticking up in the air in the bushes. I thought it was a pheasant, because I had seen a few flying around the dam which was located below our tent, at the foot of the hill. I decided to sneak up and catch this pheasant. I tip-toed, and started to make a grab. I froze when I saw that it wasn't a bird, but an agama which is a type of lizard, like an iguana. It was large, and it had brilliant colors. It turned its head, and its long tongue kept spitting out at me. My legs were weak, and I couldn't move. It was so big, and its fat legs were bowed. It finally moved away from me. I thought I had run into a small dinosaur.

I lounged around all day. There was nothing happening. It started to get dark, and I was getting worried. It was awfully scary at night to be left alone by myself. I was going to play it safe, so I went up above our tent. The road was a very narrow one that ended about fifty feet above our tent. Along one side of the road was a ditch. I figured that the safest place to be would be in the ditch. I could challenge anyone first. We had a password which every Marine knew.

While I was in the ditch, I saw a large figure walking down the path. I waited until he was about ten feet away, and I cocked my rifle, and hollered, "What's the password?!" He dove into the bushes, and I could hear him fleeing. I fired my rifle into the air. I didn't want to kill him.

One reason for this was that someone had said that there was an Army radar station up on the hilltop, and I wouldn't want a mistake like that on my mind. I fired a few more shots into the air then I heard the jeep, loaded with my buddies. They were yelling, "We're coming Pete! What's happening?"

"Thanks a lot, pals, I replied."

"We knew you could handle things up here, they said."

I was happy I never fired my rifle at who ever was there. I could have shot him dead. The phone in the tent rang, and the caller asked if we needed help. I assured him that everything was OK.

While up in the hills, we ran across small patches of garden, planted with tomato plants and green beans. I knew that they were not somebody's "Victory Garden".

After a few weeks, we were relieved from the ammunition post, and we rejoined our battery. Sharp Kosanke said he was glad that I was back. I was sitting on my sack, and all at once, something hit me on the back of the neck, and hung down the front of my chest. I grabbed it, and I almost jumped out of my skin. It was a dead snake. I heard laughing outside of my tent. They got quite a charge out of that, and they said it was to welcome me back.

When we had been back about a week, Major Dewey and Lieutenant Ryan picked our gun crew for a special assignment. It seemed that a big bypassed island, possibly Babeeur, was still occupied by the Japanese.

This bypassed island was supposed to be better fortified than Peleliu. It was located somewhere between Angaur and Peleliu in the Palau group. They had large artillery guns along the hillside, and they kept firing during the day into the harbor where our ships were anchored. Then they would disappear. There was a small islet less than a mile across the channel from that large island. Their idea was for us to set up a 90mm anti-aircraft gun along the shore of the islet, and to keep firing at the island to try to make them fire back. Then, the Navy could pinpoint their location, and bombard them with their sixteen-inch projectiles.

We were transported to the islet aboard an LST. The Marines assigned to this mission were Sharp Kosanke, Roy Hoover, John Blanchard, Fulgentiz, Bill Higgins, William J. Keller, Jr., J.M. Kelly, Zeke Davis, Austin A. Sapp, Earl Cole, Vincent Norton, Alex Evenly, James Greenwood, and me.

The small islet was not occupied by the Japanese, and it was safe. No problem. We landed, and reassured ourselves by covering the whole islet. As everything was being set up, such as our tents and our cots, we could see the Japanese across the channel, and they could see us. Our 90mm gun was set in place, and we unloaded tons of ammunition. The next morning, we started shelling. We were firing at least twenty-two rounds per minute. We kept firing at random for most of the day to whatever area we selected. The next day, we were given the target by a Piper Cub plane which was spotting for us, and we could see little splashes in the channel about one hundred feet away.

In the morning, they would go swimming, and they would wave towels at us. Then one morning, we gave them a big surprise. We fired a few rounds along the beach and they never waved towels after that.

We had quite a time. Often, if there was an excessive amount of firing, I could see blood coming out of the gunner's glove. I had seen this happen to our gunner at times on Eniwetok. I saw this happening again while we were shelling. I was the loader. I would place the shell in the chamber, and the gunner, with his fist on the cap end of the shell, would ram it into the chamber, and pull the lanyard. That would trigger the gun. I told the gunner that I would take the shell out of the fuse box, and load it all the way into the chamber with one motion. All he had to do was pull the lanyard. This way I was able to load an average of twenty-two rounds per minute.

One day, just for fun we located a big tree on top of the hill across the channel, and we decided to fire an armor-piercing projectile to see if we could hit it. Our good range finders lined up the barrel, and we fired. We hit it right in the middle of the trunk. We heard and watched it split right down the middle. It was no longer the highest tree on the hillside.

In spite of all the pounding on that island, the Japanese never would fire back, but we did keep them from firing at our ships in the harbor.

We were relieved by another gun crew, and we were shipped back to Angaur. On the way back to our camp, we saw a large tent. Outside, there was a large generator sending power to electric lights strung up inside the tent. We saw a bunch of natives inside the tent. The Navy had shipped in about ten washing machines and the native women were so fascinated, that they kept washing their clothes over and over. Previously, they had been washing their clothes along the beach by beating them with paddles. We wondered who would service the machines if the war ended, and would they leave enough fuel to run the generators?

Then we heard about the invasion of Iwo Jima. We wondered where Iwo Jima was. They had said on the radio, that it was an island in the East China Sea, just seven hundred fifty miles from Tokyo. Airfields there could become a base for an American assault on Japan. Our buddies said that while we were gone, the Corps was looking for volunteers for Iwo Jima, because they had sustained heavy losses, but no one volunteered.

I hadn't been back for a week when I drew guard duty for an outpost close to the ocean. There was a guard post erected there which looked like an outhouse with the top screened in. I could see in all directions from the post. It was pretty much wooded on two sides, but I could seen nothing but water on the other side.

Getting guard duty during the day wasn't bad at all. Some of the men would come down and swim in the ocean. It was really something to see schools of dolphins and porpoises looking like they were patrolling the shoreline. They would dive into the water in unison, and come out about every ten feet, still in unison. It was a beautiful sight.

But at night, it was much different. It was very dark. I could see the moon glaring on the water, and I had the feeling that some Japanese soldier was watching me from the wooded area. It was the worst four hours that any person could go through. I knew that all the men hated this outpost, but they kept it to themselves. After all, we were not supposed to be scared, or at least, we were not supposed to show it. The main camp was about a mile away from that outpost. Many times at night, I would hear rifle fire coming from the direction of that outpost. Four Marines would jump into a jeep, and within minutes, they would be at the outpost.

"What happened?"

"Oh, I thought I saw movement in the bushes", or "I heard noise," the lonely Marine would say.

I always seemed to get that extra special guard duty. Early one evening, while I was on duty, about ten of my buddies dropped in for a visit. It seemed as if our water purification system had one hundred fifty octane gasoline running through its distillation unit. A fifty-gallon drum of gasoline would make about two gallons of high proof alcohol and a little bit of it would make my hair stand up. They had two quarts of the stuff, and a couple of cans of grapefruit juice that they mixed with it. They were having a good time, but I was on duty, and I couldn't drink. They said that they would wait for me to be off duty. They were singing and having a good time.

I'd think, "How can a bunch of men have a good time just by drinking on a jungle island?" Well, we would bring up certain incidents that happened in the past that were particularly funny, and they caused laughter. Once, in the Russell Island, there was a Marine who was fed up, and he wanted to go back to the States. His bright idea was that he could pretend for the major that he thought he might be a homosexual. He walked into the major's quarters, and he told the major that it was getting to the point where he couldn't stand the sight of a naked man. The major pulled down his pants, exposed himself, and said "What does this do to you?" The Marine ran out of the quarters, and nothing ever became of the incident.

We also laughed about the two men who wanted a discharge, and actually pretended to be homosexual. They tossed a coin to see which one would be on top. They waited for the sergeant to do a bed check. They timed it right. The sergeant walked in and caught them. They did get a discharge and it was the first time that I had seen a military court-martial. They were placed in the brig. When the paperwork was ready, our whole company was lined up like we were going to have a full dress parade. The prisoners were in front, facing the whole battalion. The major read the charges, and gave a description of exactly how it happened. We though it was funny, but they were stripped of all Marine insignias. Even the Marine emblem on the pocket was torn off and they both received a bad conduct discharge. We thought how unfortunate it was, after being overseas, and going through the worst part, that they would have to explain themselves years later.

We laughed about another incident. It happened on Eniwetok. One fellow loved to sleep naked. Whenever we had cots to sleep on, he slept on his stomach. He was warned to sleep with some clothes on, but he wouldn't listen. Big Freeman, whom we called Alabama, was about six feet-five inches tall, and we kidded him that we wouldn't team up with him to dig a foxhole, because we didn't have a ladder to climb out of it. Well, he came up with an idea that would break the naked Marine's habit. He got a broom and twirled it between the cheeks of the naked man's rear, and quickly dropped it. That made the sleeping beauty roll over fast. He looked up and saw Alabama standing over him. We all laughed. It cured his habit of sleeping naked.

Another funny incident had happened on Eniwetok. A Seabee was selling good whiskey for thirty dollars a bottle. Frank Kwiatkowski and I agreed to meet near the mess hall after dark. He was to make the deal. The Seabee walked up to the mess hall, and asked Frank if he had the money. He handed Frank the bottle, and I surprised him with "What's going on here?!" I was dressed with an MP band on my arm. The Seabee took off running, and we had a free bottle of good whiskey. Men were looking for activity, and getting restless. One evening, I heard commotion in the tent next to mine. I knew that the men were drinking, so I went over to see what the commotion was about. Leo Sisco, an Indian Marine, had Joe Crovo in a choke hold, and Crovo's tongue was hanging out. I grabbed Sisco from the back, and tried to force his arms apart, but he wouldn't budge. He kept saying, "I'm going to choke you!" I picked him up, and we both rolled over a cot. He started to swing at me, but he kept missing because he was loaded. Crovo was very much shaken up by the incident. Sisco was so loaded, that he fell asleep on the floor of the tent. We made sure that Sisco didn't drink after that. In a sadder incident, two Marine buddies got into an argument, one pulled out his rifle, and shot his buddy dead. When he sobered up, he wanted to kill himself. He was in the brig, waiting for deportation back to the States. I drew guard duty to guard him. The brig was a tent with barbed wire around it. He had to be guarded twenty-four hours a day. The eves on the tent were rolled up. I checked behind the roll, and found a bunch of razor blades. He wasn't violent, but he was a very sad Marine. During the period in which I guarded him, he kept saying that it must have been an accident, and that he would never shoot his best friend. The other Marines in the tent that saw the whole thing disagreed, however. Both men had been drinking, and the argument started over a "Dear John" letter that the one Marine had received from home. His buddy kept telling him that his girlfriend wasn't worth much dropping him like that, and that she had probably been cheating on him all along. Their liquor was doing most of the talking when the word "whore" got into the conversation. That ended it!

With time to spare, and no reassignment, men started to get bored, so Lieutenant Ryan, who was a great sportsman, started to organize sports activities. We had fast pitch softball teams. Quite a few men from the western states played professional fast pitch softball. Lieutenant Ryan organized basketball teams, and he scheduled a big track meet. Our battalion also had a traveling softball team. Lieutenant Ryan and Second Lieutenant Phillips had tryouts, and I made the team. I had never played fast pitch softball before, so the game was new to me and I found out that it was not so easy as it seemed.

Finally, we were put on a new training program. Each day, we marched up to a cleared training area. We were learning how to make pipe bombs. We had new flame throwers. The range of these flame throwers was determined by how much pressure one placed upon the trigger. After watching some of the fellows ahead of me, I was going to get the maximum distance when my turn came. I would show them. "OK, LaCivita. Your turn." Everyone was standing behind me. I gave the trigger a fast, hard squeeze. The kick from the flame thrower shot up into the air. Everyone scattered. The trigger was stuck, and it wouldn't shut off. I told everyone to move further back out of range. I had to hold the flame thrower until all the fuel was burned out of it. My face was as red as a beet. I didn't panic, but I was scared. It finally burned out. I must have jammed the trigger.

We were also being trained for street fighting. We were moving away from jungle tactics. We were told that we probably would be going back to Camp Lejeune, New River, North Carolina, where the Seventh Armored Division was being formed. It would be one of the first to invade the Japanese homeland.

One thing that I would miss on this island was a little Catholic church. It looked like a miniature cathedral, holding no more than twenty-five people. It had a balcony that held ten people. It was a white stucco building set in among some palm trees. Bill Lawrence and I used to go early so we could get a seat in the balcony.

In mid April, we received news by word of mouth that there was a radio announcement stating that our Commander-in-Chief, Franklin D. Roosevelt, had died. We felt bad, and we wondered how this development would affect the war. We heard that the new president was Harry S. Truman, and that he reaffirmed FDR's commitment: "No peace until unconditional surrender!" Shortly afterward, on May 7, 1945, we received word that the Germans had surrendered. In the Pacific, we still had plenty of fighting to do, and we felt that the worst was still to come.

By June, most of the men were anxious to move on. We felt that we were being wasted on the island. In order to keep in shape and to keep occupied, we went through the hills again, looking for Japanese holdouts. We checked caves. We threw a lot of grenades into the caves, but we didn't find it necessary to go inside them. Most of them were built out of concrete, and they went a great distance into the hillsides.

Our ammunition, which was stored on the island, had to be moved, so our battalion detailed two "gangs" to the U.S.S. Alamosa, an ammunition carrying ship. The ocean conditions were very unfavorable, which caused the various vessels to pitch. They became unstable platforms from which to work. There were heavy rains and strong winds. The job was hazardous because sensitive control of the ammunition and explosives were required. I would line up five hundred pound bombs, making sure that there was support between the bombs so that they wouldn't roll. Below deck, there was a very dim lighting, and the ship kept rocking back and forth. We had seen the ship that blew up at Eniwetok, so we knew how careful we had to be. We had two gangs, which alternated working below deck and above deck, unloading smaller vessels. There was a commissioned officer who worked alongside us. We got along well with the officers and men of the Alamosa. They thought that it was a lousy job that we had been given, but we were proud to do it. Our commanding officer, Elmer C. Woods, was notified by F.M. Hillman, skipper of the Alamosa, of our behavior and discipline and received a letter of congratulations.

We were always located near an airstrip. Many fighters and bombers would return from their missions all shot up, and limp in to land. Many bombers would come in on only two or three engines. One B-24 Liberator come in on only one engine and we cheered as if the pilot could hear us. He made a perfect landing. The crew was able to hear us as they exited the plane.

But one day a buddy and I were watching a B-24 take off for a bombing mission. The plane started down the runway, got up about ten feet into the air and crashed. We went running toward the crash. The exit door flew open, and the crew members jumped out. An airman said that the copilot was dead, but the pilot was pinned in with a rod through his arm, and that we needed an ax to get him out. The plane didn't explode, but one of the engines was burning. Without thinking, my buddy and I started into the plane to see what we could do. Then we heard a major screaming at the top of his lungs, "Move away from the plane if you don't want a court-martial! It's loaded with bombs!" All we could think about was the pilot dying a slow death as we followed his order. The plane was engulfed in flames, with lots of black smoke, and then it blew. I thought, if only something could have been done to save the pilot. After the fact, we were glad that the major put some sense in our heads but I wondered if we had gone in, if we could have saved that pilot!

The invasion of Okinawa was on Easter Sunday, April 1, 1945. The fighting lasted close to three months, and we heard that twelve thousand Americans lost their lives.

The invasion of Iwo Jima brought the war in the Pacific closer to Japan. With the Marianas occupied, our B-29 Superfortress bombers were within striking distance of their homeland. We no longer had any purpose on Angaur in the Palau Islands, so we made preparations to leave. The Seventh Anti-Aircraft Battalion was disbanded, and all of the men who had been overseas before Pearl Harbor were transferred to the Twelfth Defensive Battalion to fill the vacancy which would be created by some of those men leaving with us. We were going to be part of the group of Marines going to Camp Lejeune in North Carolina to help make up the new Seventh Armored Division.

We all embarked aboard the U.S.S. Grundy, APA 111, at Angaur, in the Palau Island, on July 39, 1945. We sailed from there on the same day. Our troop commander was First Lieutenant George P. Shultz. We were a jubilant bunch of troops, finally going back to the States. I had been overseas for two years, and I was anxious to get home and see my family. We didn't know if we would be reporting to Camp Lejeune first, or if we were going home on leave. Either way would have suited me fine. We enjoyed the trip, but we still couldn't be careless out at sea. The Japanese could have still had submarines in the Pacific. We had an escort which consisted of a sub chaser and a couple of light cruisers.

Each day, we got closer to home. Some of the men were playing cards, and others were shooting dice, but most of us were lounging on the deck. Everyone was joyous. Bill and I still slept on deck at night as much as possible. We did a lot of star gazing. We pretended to look at the star shining over our house back at home.

chapter

Goodbye Friends – A Job Well-done!

I was standing near a water fountain, filling up my canteen, when I heard over the ship's loudspeaker system that an atomic bomb had been dropped on Hiroshima, Japan, and that it had wiped out the whole city. We couldn't believe that one bomb could do that! They kept giving us the latest news over the loudspeaker system as they received it. They talked about a B-29 bomber that had taken off from an island in the Marianas with a big bomb. The whole ship was buzzing about the bomb, and how it had leveled the whole city with a big mushroom-like explosion. We didn't sleep that night. All we thought about was the big bomb.

The next day, we heard that President Harry S. Truman had given the order to drop the bomb, and that he told the Japanese to surrender, or another city would be wiped out with another bomb. Then, the second bomb was dropped on Nagasaki. We all cheered on board the ship. None of us wanted to see the Seventh Armored Division, or the invasion of Japan. We anchored at Pearl Harbor, but we did not disembark. We were told that we would be going back to the States.

Halfway back to the States, on August 14, 1945, we heard that Japanese officials were on the U.S.S. Missouri, preparing to surrender. Victory at last! Thank you, President Harry Truman, for a wise decision. We believed that the Japanese would have prolonged the war for many months, and that would have costed a million or more lives on both sides. We found out later that the name of the bomber was the Enola Gay.

We arrived at San Diego, California, on August 19, 1945. As the tug boats were pulling our ship in, we could see a large crowd of people along the shore and on the dock. We were the first troops from the Pacific to come in to dock as the war came to an end. The band was playing, and people were cheering. What a beautiful sight! We disembarked at the same spot where I had embarked upon the Bloemfontein. As we walked down the gang plank, women were passing out cartons of fresh milk and candy. We were getting hugs and kisses from all the women. We received a royal welcome.

We were loaded onto military trucks, and driven to Camp Elliot, California. We were housed in the barracks, and we were told that we would be staying there for about a week before we went home. Also, we would be given our new orders.

Before we went to eat at the mess hall, we were told that we could fill our trays with whatever we desired. We would be serving ourselves. We had to remember, however, that our eyes would be bigger than our stomachs, and if we stuffed ourselves too much, we could develop appendix problems. When we went to the mess hall, I had never seen so much food. They had roast beef, chicken, turkey, and pork chops, along with corn-on-the-cob, mashed potatoes, french fries, and baked potatoes. Everyone coming through the line had their trays, which were each about fifteen inches wide and twenty inches long, stacked with everything. For dessert, they had fruit pies, cream pies, chocolate cake, yellow cake, and white cake. The amount of food was unbelievable! We all ate like pigs, and we couldn't stop laughing, seeing everyone eat. At breakfast, it was the same way. There was hot cereal, cold cereal, eggs the way one liked them, hot cakes, and waffles. Whatever we couldn't eat on our trays was taken outside. I couldn't believe my eyes when I saw fifty-five gallon drums loaded to the top with perfectly good discarded food. It didn't take but a few meals before we all came to our senses, and realized the amount of food that we were wasting.

We were made to go to table manners classes. We were taught how to use a knife, fork, and spoon, how to cut meat in a dish, and how to eat soup with a spoon, and not drink it down. We must have developed bad eating habits that we were not aware of.

Because we were quarantined to the base, we had plenty of time on our hands. I wrote a letter to L.C. Stapley and family in Sandy, Utah, thanking them for the post card with a prayer on it, which I found in my ditty bag when I boarded the ship to first go overseas. I kept the prayer with me in my wallet and believed that the post card with the prayer kept God watching over me. I received a letter back, and I was sorry to hear the bad news. Mr. L.C. Stapley, who was a preacher, had passed away one month before his family received my letter.

We received our sea bags, and we were to take them home with us. We turned our weapons in but we could keep any Japanese souvenirs that we had. Some of the men had Japanese money, and things that they had removed from dead Japanese soldiers, but I didn't want any of that stuff. But we got a big laugh from a Marine from New Jersey who could hardly carry his sea bag. He was a small fellow as it was. We asked, "What the hell do you have in there?" He was trying to smuggle his machine gun home. He had the machine gun in the center of the bag, with blankets and clothes stuffed around it.

We finally got our orders, and our transportation tickets were given to us. I would be going home on leave, but I had to report to the First Guard Company Marine Base, at the Navy Yard in Philadelphia, Pennsylvania. We were happy to be going home, but in a way it was sad. These were men whom I had met as strangers. But it wasn't long until we became buddies and pals, and treated one another as brothers. We had never let each other down. We were always a team. We had happy times, good times, sad times, and hard times. When we shared packages from home, the receiver generally got the least, trying to make sure that all the buddies got some. Guys like Buddy Fugentiz, whose parents owned a grocery store in Long Island, New York. They always mailed large packages, and we enjoyed every one of them.

From the time that I entered the Marine Corps, until the time that I was discharged, I never heard of any money or personal items being stolen. Wherever we were housed, be it in a barracks or a tent, I could always leave my wallet sitting in my sack or foot locker. One could leave one's personal items out. I never heard of anything being stolen. That's the kind of friendship and character that I found in the Marine Corps.

Before we all left one another, three Marines had borrowed a few bucks from me, and they said that they would repay me. They were from different states. The men were Frank J. Sardo from New Britain, Connecticut; Ray T. Hoover from Williamsport, Maryland; and a fellow named Payne. It wasn't much money, so I told them not to bother, and to just forget it. I was surprised to get Christmas cards from two of them, with the money inside. The other one mailed me a thank you note, along with the sum he had borrowed. These men knew that the chances of seeing me again would be slim. I was going to miss all of them, and I would never forget them.

Quite a few of us would still be together from San Diego to Chicago, where most of us would head in different directions. We boarded the train in San Diego. We were assigned to pullman cars. All of our clothes were cleaned and pressed, and we all looked sharp again. All the people along the way waved and cheered and held up American flags. We could feel the jubilation of the people, especially at railroad stations.

From San Diego to Chicago, we traveled in a troop train. We were going in different directions, but some of the men were left in San Diego. They were in the hospital because they had developed appendicitis, and they had to have their appendixes removed due to the overeating. Those men would be delayed for several weeks.

The train had a two hour delay in one of the western states, and we were given permission to leave the train. The engineer would blow the whistle five minutes before the train was to pull out of the station. That would be our signal to get back on. We walked around the town, bought cigarettes, gum, and candy, and ate ice cream cones. The whistle blew, and a couple of my buddies and I ran as fast as we could, and we just made it. We learned that two of the men had missed the train. We were worried about them. Then, about four hours later, at the next stop, we saw them standing on the platform, waiting to board the train again. They were smart enough to have gone to a private airport, to have found out where the train's next layover would be, and to have hired an air taxi to fly them to that stop.

Everyone was anxious to get home. Most of the talk was about girls. In the Pacific, all we could do was dream about them. Sure, we had our pinup girls, but I recall having gone one year without seeing a woman. It had been so bad that on Eniwetok, when Bob Hope gave his performance, there were several women with him. A Marine had come running through camp, shouting that a girl had just stepped off of a plane on the airstrip. It looked like an invasion. We were running from tree to tree. I heard, "Look! She's standing by the plane. So that's what a real woman looks like!" Just seeing her made our day. Boy, it was good to see girls again!

We finally boarded the train from Chicago to Pittsburgh. On our arrival there, we were greeted by two long lines of people who made way for us to walk up the middle. It was chilling when I saw my mother and father waiting for me. It was about ten o'clock at night, and they had been waiting for three hours, watching servicemen come in on different trains. One of my brothers, Tony was with them. He had just been drafted, and was scheduled to go into the Army the next week.

It was a joyous ride back home to East McKeesport. When we arrived, the house was filled with neighbors. It was nice to see how much my youngest brother, Mike, and youngest sister, Margie, had grown since I was gone. My brother Lou was still in Europe, but married sister Lucille was at home because her husband, George, was still in the Pacific; and sisters, Mary and Josephine, were home, too.

That evening, my mother cooked a large pot of spaghetti with meatballs and sausage. My dad had a few barrels of wine in the cellar.

The next morning, my mother told me to go to the back of the house, and look in the chicken coop. When I got there, I saw two very large turkeys. They must have each weighed about thirty pounds. My mother said, "See those turkeys? On Sunday, we're eating yours. The other one is for Louie when he comes home." When I left for the service, she had some chickens, and a few turkeys. During the war years, because of meat rationing, my family consumed most of them. My mother, however, kept two turkeys for my brother Louie and me. The turkeys were to stay alive until we came home. If we had stayed away for another year, those turkeys might have each weighed forty pounds!

I took a walk through town, expecting to meet old friends. While I was standing near the bus stop, my neighbor friend John Schaeffer got off of the bus. He was surprised to see me. "Pete, let's stop in at Jake's Tavern."

"OK, let's do that," I said. That tavern was filled with hometown friends. John had not been home for about three years. He was one of the first draftees into the Army. We entered the bar at about three o'clock in the afternoon. In a spirit of celebration, everyone kept buying us drinks, until he couldn't stand up.

During my two weeks of leave at home, my sisters' girlfriends' visits became more frequent, and I had some dates. My dad had made sure that my 1941 Ford, which was housed in the garage, was in fine shape. Lots of friends kept coming home, and we had to celebrate every time, but no matter what time I got in, my mother would still be waiting for me.

On September 10. 1945, when my leave time was up, I reported to the Marine Base Navy Yard in Philadelphia. When I reported in, Captain Baileu said that I was part of the First Guard Company. My duty consisted of checking the identity of personnel entering the Navy Yard. One nice thing was that I could leave the base without a pass when I was off duty.

I was sent to the hospital from there to have the coral growth between my toes removed. I couldn't believe my eyes when I saw a Marine with no arms or legs coming down the hall in a wheelchair, being pushed by a nurse. My heart just left me. Marines and Sailors in wheelchairs were everywhere. Some had two arms, but no legs; some had one leg; some had one leg and one arm. It was a sight I would never forget. I became friends with a couple of patients. One patient said that some didn't want their families to ever see them again. Men who were facially deformed would never leave the Veteran's Hospital. I was somewhat ashamed to tell my friend why I was there.

I prepared for surgery. I lay on top of metal table which looked like it came from a morgue. I was on my back, with both of my feet sticking up. A nurse gave shots to both of my afflicted toes. As the doctor cut the coral growth out, I could feel the knife cutting, but I remained calm by thinking about the men in the wheelchairs.

Before I left Philadelphia, I received my discharge. While one was in the service, every officer one served under would mark an evaluation sheet as follows:

(0) Bad
(1) Indifferent
(2) Fair
(3) Good
(3.8) Very Good
(4.3-5) Excellent

Ratings were given for:
Military efficiency
Neatness and Military Bearing
Intelligence
Obedience
Sobriety
Average Standing

My average score was 4.5. My ratings as a specialist in special duty details were excellent according to U.S.M.C. Major J. S. Dewey. I was discharged on November 3, 1945.

I was finally home for good, and the first month was just one big party. My brother Lou came home from Europe, and my brother-in-law, George Lokay was discharged from the Army.

More than sixteen million Americans had served in uniform in World War II by the time it officially ended on December 31, 1946. America was jubilant. We were welcomed home with kisses, confetti, and ticker tape parades. We traded in our uniforms for civilian clothes, looking forward to the future. Our dreams had become real.

But for the 406,000 men and women who had lost their lives, there was no chance for a future, let alone freedom. There was no happiness for their families. Many of these casualties were buried at sea, and many are still buried overseas. Most of their bodies were shipped home by rail.

In large cities and small towns alike, there were many military funerals. One could see a funeral procession with military honors each day. There were many tearful families. The "killed in action" letters were followed by the return of the bodies. I was asked by the local Marine Corps Reserve Unit to participate in the Military Honor Guard. I became one of a group assigned to stand guard over caskets, which had to be guarded until the time of burial. A picture of the service person would be placed on top of the casket. It was very hard for me to keep my composure while I watched the families viewing the caskets with their loved ones inside. A few would always question how they could be sure that their son was in the casket.

I had the privilege of being a pallbearer for two of my local high school friends. Walter Kozak, who had served with the Air Force, was killed by shrapnel from anti-aircraft flak while flying over Italy. Harold Hess was killed in action during the invasion of Guam.

The road to victory cost many lives. When I was standing over a slain serviceman's casket, I realized the tremendous loss which was bestowed upon families. The empty chair at the dinner table, the remembrance every Christmas of the stocking which used to hang above the fireplace, the memories mom had of waking him up for school, and dad of watching him play sports. The mothers received gold stars, but they were left with incurable wounds.

These are the only things left now after fifty years and most of these parents are gone. I hope that our future generations will be reminded that our American freedom did not come cheaply, but with faith, honor, hope and even life itself.

The End

Recognition

7th Defense/AAA Battalion Assn.
U.S. Marine Corps.
12747 Huntingwick
Houston, TX 77024

10th Defense/AAA Battalion Assn.
U.S. Marine Corps
276 Northgate Ave.
Daly City, CA 94015 & 22nd Marine Division

U.S. Marine Base
"A" Battery Artillery Bn. T.C.
Camp Lejeune
New River, NC

U.S. Marine Base
Ordinance School
Quantico, VA

U.S. Marine Base
10th Recruit Battalion
Parris Island, SC

Marine Corps League
Hesse Waltron Detachment
East McKeesport, PA 15035

Marine Corps League
P.O. Box 3070
Merrifield, VA 22116

LAMENT OF A 10TH DEFENSE BATTALION AAA CREW
somewhere in the South Pacific
(written in the Solomons 50 odd years ago
& was published in the Leatherneck)
PFC John "Tony" Anthony

The day is almost over.
The sun is sinking fast.
Marines begin to gather for
Tonight may be their last.

It's a perfect night for bombing
We know they will be here soon.
You hear a Gyrene whisper-man,
I wish there was no moon.

Then there it is, the horns blast;
The signal that they're hear at last.
We hit the deck, make a run,
Grab our gear, man our guns.

We stand there tense, ready for action.
Each man knows, what's going to happen.
We watch our lights sweep the heavens,
Then there it is, the Mitsubishi 97.

Six men to every gun,
Each one knows what has to be done.
We wait for orders, here they come,
We open fire with all our guns.

A blinding flash, a deafening roar;
The first shots off and followed by more.
So let'em come, sound out the taps,
For we'll lay our 90's square in their laps.

Then cease firing, and all is quiet,
We listen for bombs from out of the night.
Here they come, we all duck low,
But they miss again, with their whole damn load.

We fire again, again and again,
For we've come this far, and we are going to win.
Then there it is, a beautiful sight,
Like a fiery ball out of the night.

We laugh and yell, some of us shout,
Shamo pilot, you're out of the fight.
Tho' he tried his best, it wasn't enough,
For we're much better men than any they've got.

Now dawn arrives, a beautiful sight,
For it means we have survived another night.
With guns secure, we hit our sacks,
To get our rest for tonights attack...

APPENDIX

The U.S.S. Grundy and the Indianapolis

HERMAN DE LUCENAY - in a speech to the San Diego Reunion Banquet - described the trip home for many of us from Angaur to San Diego. DE LUCENAY expanded on the report, History of the U.S.S. Grundy, which says: "At 0945 on the 30th (July) a submarine periscope was sighted off the starboard quarter; went to general quarters and took evasive maneuvers - no further action developed. Arrived at Guam on the 31st where the prisoners of war were disembarked..."DE LUCENAY speculated that the Japanese submarine was waiting for a bigger kill, which came in the from of the Indianapolis. On that July 30th Japanese torpedoes sank the cruiser; 800 men out of the crew of 1200 made it into the water, but only 316 survived to make it home. In a newspaper article furnished by DE LUCENAY, one survivor tells of the five days of hell in the water, watching shipmates die from delirium and listening to the anguished cries of others being devoured by sharks. Both the Grundy and the Indianapolis material have been put in the permanent files.

Tenth Defense Battalion
First Marine Amphibious Corps
FMF_Pacific

22 October, 1944

Memoranda to all hands:

Today the transfer of officers and men to the "States" and to other units will begin. On the occasion of your departure, all thoughts are undoubtedly of the days to come whether they are to be in the "States" or in a new phase of the war. However, as you complete this tour of duty you should not fail to look back with pride on the record which you have helped this battalion to build.

It is a fine record. You successfully and smartly performed every mission. You successfully protected all ships, planes and military installations which it was your duty to defend. You disrupted enemy attacks, destroyed their aircraft and killed their flying personnel. In spite of their repeated efforts, the Japs (sic) were able to destroy nothing entrusted to your care.

I personally regret that it was not my privilege to serve with you in the more active days. I am glad to have been with you during these past months, to have commanded you, and to have observed your many soldierly qualities.

There are tests as trying for a man-or an outfit-as active combat. That is particularly true of the type of duty we have done. The alert manner in which you carried on tedious tasks over a long period of time has demonstrated unusual pride and devotion to duty. When you arrived here you did not let down but have continued to present a standard of conduct and appearance that has attracted the attention and favorable comment of the camp commander, civilians and of other commanding officers.

I am proud of you. Continue to be proud of yourselves and to demonstrate that pride in your work, your manner and your bearing wherever you may serve in the future.

Good luck to you all.

Thomas G. Roe
Lt. Col
10th Def. Bn
Kauai, T.H.

One of the many letters our Bn. received

The Secretary of the Navy
Washington

The Secretary of the Navy takes pleasure in commending the

Twenty-Second Marines, Reinforced, Tactical Group One, Fifth Amphibious Corps

consisting of

Twenty-second Marines; Second Separate Pack Howitzer Company; Second Separate Tank Company: Second Separate Engineer Company; Second Separate Medical Company; Second Separate Motor Transport Company; Fifth Amphibious Corps Reconnaissance Company; Company D, Fourth Tank Battalion, Fourth Marine Division; 104th Field Artillery Battalion, U.S. Army; Company C, 766th Tank Battalion, U.S. Army; Company A, 708th Amphibian Tank Battalion, U.S. Army; Company D. 708th Provisional Amphibian Tractor Battalion, U.S. Army; and the Provisional DUKW Battery, Seventh Infantry Division, U.S. Army.

for service as follows:

"For outstanding heroism in action against enemy Japanese forces during the assault and capture of Eniwetok Atoll, Marshall Islands, from February 17 to 22, 1944. As a unit of a Task Force, assembled only two days prior to departure for Eniwetok Atoll, the Twenty-second Marines, Reinforced, landed in whole or in part on Engebi, Eniwetok and Parry Islands in rapid succession and launched aggressive attacks in the face of heavy machine-gun and mortar fire from well camouflaged enemy dugouts and foxholes. With simultaneous landings and reconnaissance missions on numerous other small islands, they overcame all resistance within six days, destroying a known 2,665 of the Japanese and capturing 66 prisoners. By their courage and determination, despite the difficulties and hardships involved in repeated reembarkations and landing from day to day, these gallant officers and men made available to our forces in the Pacific Area an advanced base with large anchorage facilities and an established airfield, thereby contributing materially to the successful conduct of the war. Their sustained endurance, fortitude and fighting spirit throughout this operation reflect the highest credit on the Twenty-second Marines, Reinforced, and on the United States Naval Service."

All personnel attached to and serving with any of the above units during the period February 17 to 22, 1944, are authorized to wear the Navy Unit Commendation Ribbon.

"To the 10th Defense Battalion:

Eniwetok Atoll – Entitled to Bronze Star for occupation of Eniwetok Atoll 17 February to March 2, 1944.

signed Edwin H. Wienicke,
Capt., USMC.

1st Japanese territory taken from the enemy by forces of the United Nations."

From : Commanding Officer.
To : Commanding Officer, Seventh Anti-Aircraft Artillery Battalion, Fleet Marine Force, Pacific.

Subject: Enlisted Marines as Stevedores.

1. From 272000K of June to about 06103K of July, in sixteen hour periods, a group of Marine Corpsmen consisting of approximately thirty-two enlisted men and a commissioned officer have loaded ammunition and other explosives into the ALAMOSA from lighters and other craft moored alongside.

2. The work has been difficult because of unfavorable sea conditions which caused the various vessels to pitch and scend becoming unstable platforms from which to work, difficult because of the necessity of careful stowage and shoring, difficult because of heavy rains and strong winds and hazardous because of, as in the case of dynamite, sensitive control of cargo movement was absolutely necessary.

3. The Seventh Anti-Aircraft Artillery Battalion detailed two "gangs" to accomplish the work and the ALAMOSA detailed six men to technically supplement the Marine Corps Units. As far as is know the Marines had no training nor practical experience in this activity. The job consisted of heavy work in muggy weather and was nothing short of menial labor. It was, simply stated, a lousy job that had to be done by men who were old timers in the Pacific and were, come the moment and transportation, homeward bounders.

4. These Marines performed a splendid job in loading the ALAMOSA. They were quick, alert and energetic, and within the limits of the experience of the author of this letter, they were by far the best of any non-technical organization so far met.

5. In their off moments, as when waiting for lighters to come alongside, the Marines lounged about the decks and mess hall of the ship. They were invariably neat, clean and orderly. The officers and men of the ALAMOSA came to enjoy their presence and something of friendships were built up.

6. The officers and men of the ALAMOSA all join in extending congratulations to those of the Seventh Anti-Aircraft Artillery Battalion.

/s/ F. M. Hillman
F. H. Hillman

Naval Support

The infantry assault units in the Marshalls operations were carried by an incredible array of ships designed to perform very specialized functions. Also included were converted destroyers. The amphibian tractors carried the invading Marines in to the beaches. supplemented by the older ramped landing craft. Added to these were a jumble of acronyms: LCI, LST, LSM, etc, for infantry, rockets, tanks, and trucks.

No landings would have been successful, however, without the crucial support of naval gunfire and aerial bombardment. The fast task force that roamed the Pacific and the support groups which stood off the island objectives were visual proof of the deadly striking power that had been reborn in the U.S. Navy in the two years since the debacle at Pearl Harbor. Nearly all the old, slow battleships which had lain shattered in the mud were back in action, and now were joined by brand new, fast counterparts, and the familiar old peacetime carriers were now supplemented by a steady flow of new fleet carriers and the innovation of smaller escort carriers.

This is the roll call of the ships which poured in their fire before and during the landings:

Battleships: *Tennessee (BB 13), Colorado (BB 45). Maryland (BB 46), Pennsylvania (BB 38), Idaho (BB 42), New Mexico (BB 40), and Mississippi (BB 41).*

Heavy Cruisers: *Louisville (CA 28), Indianapolis (CA 35), Portland (CA 33), Minneapolis (CA 36), San Francisco (CA 38), and New Orleans (CA 32).*

Light Cruisers: *Santa Fe (CL 60), Mobile (CL 63), and Biloxi (CL 80).*

Carriers: *Saratoga (CV 3), Princeton (CVL 23), Langley (CVL 28), Enterprise (CV 6), Yorktown (CV 10), Belleau Wood (CVL 24), Intrepid (CV 11), Essex (CV 9), Cabot (CVL 27), Cowpens (CVL 25), Monterey (CVL 26), and Bunker Hill (CV 17)*, plus six escort carriers.

Destroyers: *The Kwajalein Atoll* landings had 40 in direct support.

Tenth Defense Battalion
ASSOCIATION
United States Marine Corps - WWII

* *

Amoto, Anthony M.
Anthony, John J.
Arnold, Floyd
Apperson, Edward C. Capt.
Atkinson, Charles W.
Auchmoody, Lester M.
Auckett, Francis W.

Bagley, James
Banko, Basil
Barker, William P
Barnhill, Thomas E.
Beatty, J.P.
Beliah, Samuel F.
Bennett, Earnest D.
Bettin, Wesley C.
Bergmann, Barrett
Bell, H.B. 2nd Lt.
Blake, Donald W.
Blinke, Donald J.
Blanchard, John M.
Boal, James M.
Boe, Vern E.L.
Borowski, Peter W.
Boutwell, Elbert
Brewester, Norman R.
Brown, Lester H.
Brandon, Charles G.
Brandwein, Edward C.
Brown, Robert M.
Brown, John M.
Buck, Joseph L.
Burk, Orville E.
Buscaglia, Sam
Butchko, John
Banko, Bud Basil
Blackwell, Henry G.
Butova, James B.

Cackowski, Edward L.
Cavallara, Sal
Chatfield, Alvin F.
Caudill, Roosevelt
Carpenter, Charles H.
Cabral, Charles F.
Clark, Donald C.
Chew, Tilford
Ciampi, Victor J.
Cole, Earl A.
Collins, Rip
Collins, D.C.
Collins, Virgil C.
Cochran, Glenn C.
Cornell, Walter R.
Creed, Lynford
Creswell, Robert G.
Creech, Virgil N.
Cross, Curtis D.

Davis, Wilber S.
Deeter, James E.
Deithloff, Donald E.
Denney, John A.
Demarce, Bruce
Dear, Drury
De Soto, Theodore
Dewey, J.S. Major
De Voe, Edward J.
DiCostantino, John A.
Donlin, Robert J.
Duncan, Wayne D.
Dyson, James

Edwards, Vern E. Jr.
Embree, Stanley E.
Emerich, Cyril E. Major-
Comm. Officer

Fabyunskey, Frank E.
Fair, James E.
Farrell, Leonard R.
Farris, Sgt.
Fagg, Jack
Field, Robert D.
Fay, David E.
Farchild, George W.
Fejes, Arthur A.
Fornas, Gerald E.
Fetty, James R.
Foy, Dwigt E.
Foures, Joseph C.
Friel, Roland W.
Fosburg, Douglas E.
Frisbee, Jack M.
Fueller, William

Galarmeau, Maurice L.
Garner, Hershel H.
Gilbert, Dalton T.
Gibson, George W.
Giannatasio, Nicholas
Gayer, Harry Maj. General
Goldberg, Albert
Golanko, Edward
Grant, Norman W.
Greene, Edgar N.
Greenwood, James F.
Grudger, Troy C.

Harris, John H. Jr.
Handrakan, Robert J.
Hayden, Harold
Hayden, Joe
Hayes, James W.
Hayes, Howard W.
Hedgepath, James C.
Heinrich, Hayes W.
Herbst, Robert F.
Harrington, Ernest
Hegyi, Ernest S.
Higgins, William R.
Hochsmith, B.A. Major
Holman, James J.
Hood, PFC
Hoover, Roy T.
Hornek, William M.
Hrabovsky, Eugene
Hoyle, Oscar H.
Horvath, Joseph J.
Hughes, Ronald D.
Hunt, Robert H.
Hunter, Berkley
Henry, Clark G.

Inglis, Jack W.
Irwin, Wayne E.

Janulis, Arthur
Jeffery, Harold B.
Jiminey, James E.
Johnson, Herbert
Judd, James Jr.
Johnson, Harold W.

Karr, Earl
Keelin, James M.
Keil, Clarence C.
Keller, J.M.
Kelly, J.M.
Kern, Clarence J.
Koczaja, Adam R.
Kollasch, Maurice
Kog, P.J. Lt. Colonel
Kordes, Howard W.
Kraft, Kenneth P.
Kunz, Walter H.
Kwiatkowski, Frank C.

La Civita, Peter
Labbe, Raymond
La Rue, Frank C.
Limanick, Gordon L.
Lawrence, Reginald

Lawrence, William
Lelack, Thomas R.
Lee, Cleveland H.
Lee, Duane E.
Lehn, William T.
Lane, William
Lewis, Herbert E.
Lessinch, R. 2nd Lt.
Ledbetter, Walter A.
Liebenguth, Gerald
Lindsay, Glade D.
Lombard, Edward J.
Longbottom, Burton
Lucas, William J.

Mac Dougall, Gordon N.
Mac Millan, Kenneth D. Jr.
Mayor, Conrad L.
McDaniel, William R.
Manale, Joseph N.
McCay, Samuel
McIntyre, Harold A.
McKern, Chester
Meachan, Thomas
Menteer, Joseph V.
Miller, Jack
Meyer, John M.
Massar, Thomas J,.
Michael, Lt.
Momberger, Lloyd C.
Moschella, Salvatore
Moore, Stewart E. Sgt.
Mixon, C.A. Jr. Capt.
Morris, Albert B.
Morin, Walter P.
Muschinski, Herbert P.
Myers, James K.
Mizelle, Chambliss
Murphy, Paul W.

Naylor, Dick L. Jr.
Neese, Henry E.
Nelson, Marion F.
Negrey, Stephen V. Jr.
Nikels, Aubrey G.
Norton, Vincent
Novill, Robert L.
Numemacher, Claude R.

O'Donnell, John F.
O'Doherty, Constantine
O'Keefe, William
Oliver, Jack W.
Ollerman, John E.
Orr, Henry L.
Ostrowski, Alfred J.
Oyach, Henry J.

Palmer, T.C. 2nd Lt. Bn. Adj.
Parsons, Guy R.
Paschkie, Ervin A.
Parent, Albert F.
Peter, Frank V.
Pentz, Russell
Plese, John P.
Phelps, Harry W.
Pollom, Charles E.
Pierce, Jack
Piontkowski, L.J.
Prisock, Joe T.

Quinn, John T.
Quiat, Hal

Ream, Edwin K.
Reiber, George
Reed, Author A.
Reidinger, Bernard F.
Reynaud, Fredrick V.C.
Reyne, Richard M.
Richardson, Authur N.
Reutep, Raymond R.
Richards, Hershel H.
Rizzo, Peter C.
Roe, Thomas G. Lt. Col.

Ruby, Melvin T.
Rudolf, Albert H.
Ruggiero, James C.
Russo, Charles C.
Rutherford, Roger B.
Ryder, Myron W. Jr.

Sander, R.A. Capt.
Sandoval, Eloy C.
Sandifer, Thomas
Sandoval, Eloy
Sankowski, Edward
Schaner, Jim
Schmeckpeper, Ralph
Schuetz, Karl
Schwartz, Martin
Schmutz, Howard J.
Shultz, James B.
Salter, Tommie L.
Shotts, James S.
Singer, Albert J.
Sharpe, Caryle H.
Simmons, Eugene F.
Sapp, Austin A.
Sardo, Frank J.
Smith, George H.
Smith, Douglas W.
Sganga, Louis J.
Snuggs, Gary L.
Sojmosi, Thomas
Squire, Stanford Major
Stanley, Frank W.
Stelling, Victor H.
Stevens, Francis J.
Sweezy, Herbert J. Jr.
Sullivan, Robert J.
Smetana, Walter S.

Talley, Allen G. Jr.
Taylor, Joseph F.
Taylor, Fred
Tamsett, Harry A.
Tassos, George
Taylor, Ben A.
Terranova, Geno
Tedford, Albert S. Jr.
Thompson, W.O. Lt. Colonel
Tucholski, Arthur
Tweedy, Oliver B.
Turner, Henry F.
Tram, Adolph J.

Urbassik, George J.
Usher, George W.

Van Horn, William D.
Vanscicle, James W.

Waldron, Edison A.
Wareham, Jim
Warzenski, Edward J.
Wess, Howard M.
Whitefield, James T.
Whittier, Richard E.
Williamson, Lloyd. A.
Williams, Fredrich J.
Wienicke, Edward H. Capt.
Wilson, Forrest C.
Wolf, Walter P.
Wood, James A.
Woomer, Jack
Woodward, John E.

Yoke, Frank
Young, Maxwell J.

Zabkiciwich, Harry S.
Zugler, Howard

7TH DEFENSE AAA BATTALION ASSOCIATION
UNITED STATES MARINE CORPS
1940-1945

ROSTER

Abbatiello, Vincent
Adams, Edward F.
Adams, Nate L. 2nd
Adams, Note L.
Allen, Orice J.
Amicone, Mario N.
Anelick, John
Arcuri, Carmine "Jim"
Argal, James
Armstead, Robert C.
Austin, Ralph M.
Barnette, Paul J.
Baron, Robert
Barrow, Leon E.
Baugh, Wilson
Bazaman, Abe
Bell, George B.
Bennett, William A. Jr.
Benscoter, Harold M.
Betram, Harry
Bird, Farrer C.
Bird, Hugh T.
Blackburn, Victor "Blacide"
Blay, Richard G.
Blinn, John W.
Bochniarz, George
Bolerkske, Andrew G.
Border, James A.
Boston, William F.
Brackeen, McConnell
Bradt, George M.
Brandenberger, R.J. 1st Lt.
Breakfield, James W.
Briggs, Sr., A. Leon
Brisbois, D. J.
Brokaw, John A. Jr.
Broughton, Thomas B.
Buell, William A.
Burke, W. V.
Burnette, Willie N.
Burnside, John
Burns, Robert
Butta, Salvatore J.
Byrne, Frank J.
Cacchione, Phil
Calcut, Harry
Callahan, James J.
Callender, James
Cannon, Fred K.
Cardiff, Glinn
Carper, Robert G.
Cassell, Eugene H.
Cole, Earl
Branden, Charles
Cackowski, Edward
Canton, Paul E.
Chambers, John D.
Chase, Gilbert T.
Cherry, Morris R.
Chevallier, Thomas P.
Chirafisi, Carlo
Christopherson, Bruce
Cirel, Joseph
Clarke, Vince J.
Clark, Howard
Cochran, Roger L
Coggins, Thomas M.
Cohen, Eugene
Colbert, George W.
Coleman, Arron H.
Coleman, Walter C.
Coley, John P.
Collins, Geo. P
Conaghan, Thomas B.
Connizzo, Thomas D.
Corrade, Nilo
Conza, Luigi
Cordoni, Vincent
Corley, Harold T.
Cortezi, Michael J.
Crawford, Donald E.
Cromie, John H.

Crowley, Thomas L.
Cruci, Joseph E.
Cunningham, F.O.
Cyperski, Robert F.
Dahlin, Arthur L
Dangerfield, Walter L.
Daniels, William D.
Davis, Gerald
D'Amico, Louis
Crovo, Joseph L.
De Lucenay, Herman J.
Dieckmann, Edward L.
Di Geronimo, Anthony
Donn, Michael Jr.
Dewey, J.S. Major
Dodge, Steven W.
Donellan, Bernard C.
Donnell, John L. Lt. Col.
Donoghue, Bernard
Dorfachuk, Frank
Doucette, Maurice J.
Dowell, L.J.
Downs, Raymond W.
Doyle, Fred E. Jr.
Doyle, Chris W.
Blanchard, John
Davis, Zeke
Creswell, Robert
Duke, Dallas
Dunkelburger, R.B.
Dunn, William A.
Dupler, James F.
Eberly, Alex E.
Eby, Henry E.
Elder, Will M.
Engelder, Paul O.
Engelhardt, Charles
Engelhardt, Frank J.
English, Lowell
Epley, William D.
Erickson, Amory W.
Erickson, A.R.
Erickson, Edward
Erst, Adolph R.
Falkenberg, Fred J. Jr.
Farley, Terance J.
Farmer, Craig
Fayak, Joseph
Fedela, George H.
Fenty, Walter E.
Ferguson, Warren
Finch, Louis L.
Fiorellino, Dom
Follick, Robert
Forbes, Kenneth
Framer, Morris
Franklin, Claudie H.
Friend, Vernon B.
Fuirman, Alester G. 3rd
Gagner, Joseph H.
Galisin, Steve
Gibson, Herbert S.
Gillespie, Jack T.
Ginsberg, Norman E.
Gloss, James E.
Golonka, Edward
Goodheart, Kenneth R.
Goodwin, Paul
Gorman, James Jr. 2nd Lt.
Greear, Eugene W.
Gremillion, Maurice J.
Grocke, George
Groth, Arthur J.
Grubbs, Mance D.
Grzankowski, Walter S.
Grubic, Carl M.
Gudger, Troy C.
Gustafson, David N.
Guthre, Robert
Guzek, Chester S.
Hall, Lyle W.
Hall, S.L.
Hatley, John D.
Hayes, Wayne C.
Heaver, John L.
Henderson, Paul F. Jr.
Hedgepath, James
Henning, Richard
Henry, C.J. Jr.
Herms, Henry W.
Hertzog, Lewis B.
Higgins, Bill
High, Robert L.

Hills, Frank C.
Hoover, Roy
Hodge, Elmer
Holcombe, Thomas
Hollier, Emery
Hooker, Alex B.
Hough, James A.
Hovey, Milton J.
Howse, Glenn A.
Hubler, Lewis
Hughes, Walter W.
Hunter, Berkely F.
Hurley, William J.
Ingraham, Joseph F.
Ingraham, Robert E.
Irish, Hugh J.
Jett, Robert P.
Jones, Hugh E.
Keeler, William
Kelty, Morgan
Kennamer, M.J.
Kennett, Loren W.
Kent, John A.
Kelly, J.M.
Keller, William J. Jr.
Kerr, Walter J.
Kestley, Jack
Killen, George W.
Killan, William H.
King, James E.
Kipp, John D.
Kiraly, Steven
Kirsch, Jean P. Med.
Kish, Billy
Klick, Gerold S.
Klonowski, Joseph
Kolb, Vernon G.
Koprowicz, Thaddeus L.
Kosanke, Sharpe G.
Koczaja, Adam
Kries, Sherward W.
Kwiatkowski, Frank C.
LaCivita, Peter
Laban, Joseph
Lacey, George
LaHart, James H.
Langseth, Milfred A.
Larkins, Hubert M.
Lasuk, Walter
Lawrence, William
Lawson, D.
Lawton, Dick R.
Layman, Royce L.
Le Fever, Kenneth B.
Lemley, Paul F.
Leopold, James
LeVaughn, Louis J.
Levenhagen, John I.
Lewallem, James K.
Linn, Harry E.
Lipka, Fred
Lippert, Earl F.
Llewelly, Jimmy N.
Lochner, Francis J.
Lockley, Moody
Logue, Thomas C.
Low, Stanley
Lunning, Frank
Mabie, Ralph L.
Maloney, Charles
Manning, Melvin L.
Maples, Paul R.
Massar, Thomas J.
Matthews, Leon E.
McBurnett, Charles E.
McGuire, William J.
McKenzie, Thomas L.
McMullen, Patrick H.
McQuade, John
Medford, E. Leslie Jr.
Millar, Stan G.
Miller, Norman A.
Mitchell, Bryan
Mittleman, Morris
Monges, Charles J.
Montgomery, Daniel D.
Morgan, Frank G.
Mouton, Denton G.
Murray, Jack N.
Myres, William
Nadolny, George R. Jr.
Neises, Robert J.
Nessly, Jack

Newell, Neal C.
Nieciecki, Walter X
Nolan, T.J.
Norton, Vincent
Nosel, Chester T.
O'Conner, Walter
O'Doherty, C.
Odom, Joseph T.
Oliver, Carmen
Pacini, Phillip, Buck
Paige, Col.
Parker, Vann H.
Patrick, Arthur V.
Patrick, Kenneth R.
Paulini, Joseph
Peniston, Edwin T.
Petersen, Charles H.
Peterson, Thomas H.
Phillips, Harry C.
Pfaff, Karl G.
Pilet, George A.
Pinkerton, Charles Jr.
Poletis, Peter K.
Pollock, Leland H.
Powell, Ray E.
Prestwood, Dewey
Presutti, Al
Price, Joseph B.
Pugh, Ralph
Punch, George W.
Pupenko, Michael
Quandt, Robert A.
Quinn, Joseph F.
Quinn, Maurice L.
Rabin, Bernard C.
Radcliffe, C.H. Sr.
Ralphs, Theodore S.
Raquet, William H.
Reid, Odell C.
Reynolds, Bailey H.
Rheiner, Craig
Richardson, Darwin L.
Richards, Gene S.
Riley, John
Ringe, G. Truxton
Robinson, Max E.
Rood, Robert E.
Rooney, George
Rossi, Andrew F.
Roundy, Robert A.
Rubenaker, George
Ruhl, Franklin S.
Russell, John P.
Ryan, William R. 1st Lt.
Rybinski, Eugene
Sammetinger, Robert
Sanders, Alvin P.
Sanford, Carl W.
Santaniello, Antinio D.
Saucier, John L.
Sardo, Frank K.
Schmidt, William H.
Sapp, Austin A.
Scott, Joseph
Scott, Leander O.
Sealey, Thomas
Sedei, Henry
Seviregrod, Clifton
Seward, Warren
Shafer, John M.
Shapp, Al, Abraham
Sheppard, William D.
Shibla, Charles
Shipley, Harry L.
Shireman, Samuel
Shultz, George P.
Sigel, Harry D.
Simmons, David H.
Simmons, Dwight J.
Sims, George C.
Sindik, Frank
Slemp, Homer t.
Sisco, Leo J.
Shultz, George P. Troop Comm.
Smith, Andrew G. Jr.
Smith, Author E.
Smith, Jim C.
Sparks, Ernest W.
Spearman, Curtis w.
Spotts, Robert H.
Spurlock, Robert Jr.
Stahl, Robert M.
Stamper, Eugene R.
Stanley, Walter F.

Steigmann, Jerome P.
Stewart, Ray
Stillman, Charles J.
Stockwell, Stanley
Stokes, H. Britt
Strickler, Geo.E.
Stome, George
Strong, Otis R.
Stutler, Benson G.
St. Martin, Clayton D.
Sutcliffe, Fred M.
Sutton, Nicholas, J.
Sutton, Vern L.
Szczurek, Joseph F.
Szumila, Anthony D.
Taddeau, Andrew B.
Tatum, George
Taverna, Jack
Taylor, Ben. A.
Taylor, Harber L. Jr.
Taylor, Jack
Tennant, Harvey W.
Teresi, Anthony
Thomas, Holcombe H.
Tipton, William M.
Tedoran, George
Toelke, Lester
Tomaszewski, Samuel J.
Tonsky, Andrew C.
Torkelson, Frank
Tousignant, Gerald G.
Towsley, Guy V.
Tranka, Joseph
Treboniak, Al
Trimarchi, Amadeo J.
Trimarchi, Arthur G.
Tucker, Roger
Turner, Henry F.
Tyrpak, John S.
Urbansi, Walter
Utter, Howard A.
Valerte, Ray L.
Van De Walker, Robert H.
Vargas, Frank E.
Veltri, Pete J.
Ventre, Francis
Ventura, John
Verkennis, Rollance A.
Vickery, Bill J.
Volentine, John Barney
Vota, Louis L.
Walker, Edward A.
Warren Vernon VC
Warrington, Charles E.
Wenk, Dan J.
Werner, Edwin E.
Wheeler, H.P.
Wightman, Monroe L.
Wilde, Ronald
Williams, Grover C. Jr.
Wilmoth, Harry R.
Wilson, John H.
Wimbrow, John
Winegardner, Charles E.
Wire, Kenneth
Wisdo, John J. Jr.
Woods, Elmer C. Comm. Officer
Williamson, G. Jr. Capt.
Wooley, Arthur L. Jr.
Wride, Elson K.
Wright, F.E.
Young, Herman H.
Zielinski, Adam A.
Zivik, John A.
Zube, Lloyd D.
Zuckerman, Irwin S.

Later Additions to List

Bailey, Richard
Ballew, S.J. Capt.
Buscalgia, Sam
Fueller, William
Hall, W.C. Colonel
Hayden, Joe
Haydon, Harold
Kern, Clarence
Payne, J.
Salapic, J.
Fulgentiz, E.
Anderson, Vincent

Defense/AAA Battalion Additions

Audrain, Raymond
Audrain, William J.
Baileu, Captain
Baker, Elmer
Bandur, Nicholas J.
Barker, Wildred K.
Blake, Robert Col.
Biscup, Victor G.
Bottagel, Al.
Boyington, Richard
Burris, Gerald
Butler, Hal W.
Callender, James Col.
Chadwick, Frank
Chapman, Harold N.
Chatlos, Andrew
Connor, William
Copland, Lonnie L.
Davis, Warren A.
Deal, Robert W.
Deaver, Duncan C.
Denney, Howard L.
Diachenko, Louis R.
Doyle, Wilber L.
Driggers, John D.
Dugas, Wilson L.
DeVantier, Edward
Easu, Donald
Feldes, Anthony M.
Fetty, James R.
Fosbury, Douglas E.
Freeman, Grady P.
Garber, Paul W.
Garwels, Karl
Hubwer, Ernest
Godbold, Earl P.
Gosser, Verner B.
Guthrie, Robert
Haag, Philip W.
Hassinger, Frank LeR.
Hemsing, Clarence
Heinrick, Hayes W.
Hendrick, Morris
Henry, Clark G. Lt. Col.
Hettel, William O.
Hillingsworth, Paul L.
Hirsch, Melvin
Homan, Robert
Holston, James E.
Hook, Eugene E. Jr.
Hoyt, Kenneth
Hunter, Richard
Hutcheson, James E. Sr.
Infante, Nicholas
Ingrahm, Joseph F. Col.
Jackson, King F.
Jares, David V.
Jerrell, Philip
Jiminez, James F.
Johnston, Elray
Jones, H.H.
Junion, Melvin
Keller, Gene
Kicek, Stanley M.
Knapik, Edward
Kollasch, Maurice
Kordes, Howard W.
Krinok, Ellis R.
Lackner, John E.
Leffers, Robert E.
Lepley, William J.
Loe, Kenneth M.
Lucas, Dan W.
Maranto, Eugene O.
Maranto, Sam
Mareno, Robert E.
Menteer, Joseph V.
Mavor, Conrad L.
Micek, Joseph G.
Medford, E.L. Jr. Lt. Col.
Miller, Lee E.
Maher, Eugene H.
McDowell, James F.
Millar, Stanley G. Major
Mondor, Willis P.
Paige, Henry R. Col.
McMurray, Neal S.
Moore, Leo D.
Morgan, Frank G. Major
Moriarty, Edward J.
Napolitano, Lewis D.
Nauman, Walter E.
Nelson, Dean C.
Nelson, Richard J.
Nelson, Ken C.
Newbeck, Edward F. Jr.
Negley
Nix, Omar
O'Brien, John T.
O'Leary, Joseph A.
O'Leary, James M.
Oldenburg, Herbert W.
Payne, George T.
Paxton, Bill
Pearson, Carl D.
Perry, George
Petrooski, Vincent J.
Pilkington, Russ T. Jr.
Polly, Jack J.
Pollock, Harry
Pomeroy, Allen
Pratl, Joseph J.
Prehodin, Ed.
Prince, Salas J.
Prochak, Steve
Racine, William J.
Repp, Robert D.
Ribble, D. Hugh
Richardsn, John E.
Risk, Hayes
Roethel, Robert F.
Rose, Vincent J.
Rucker, Roy J.
Salzillo, John
Siegmound, Otto W.
Siesky, Marion McC.
Smolka, John
Silver, Phil.
Sorenson, B. Andrew
Sultz, James B.
Szelok, Stephen
Tatom, Albert B.
Taylor, Ben A.
Thompson, Robert F.
Thompson, William H.
Todoran, George
Torre, Charles J.
Trisch, Lewis J.
Trisch, Donald L.
Ursulan, James J.
Valentine, Robert W.
Waldon, Robert P.
Walker, Donald S.
Wagner, John A. Jr.
Walters, Robert J.
Wandrick, George
Wenyzell, Arthur
Williams, Herman W.
Wolsey, David E.
Wyant, Roy
Yarmonchic, John
Yohe, Frank
Zabkiewicz, Harry S.

Defense/AAA Battalion Additions

ındruse, R. Jose
Anderson, Vincent
Bailey, Dick
Barnes, W.E. (Jack) Col.
Bergin, Bill
Blahnik, Ted
Boroughs, Sam
Boyington, Richard
Brennan, Mark
Browley, Tom
Brownlee, Raymound
Brandon, Nick
Christo, Mort
Chapman, Harold
Chew, T.W.
Clerkin, William G.
Colninger, Bert
Cortezi, Mike Lt. Col.
Denny, Howard
Dipley, George
Dodd, W. Max
Dubensky, Paul J.
Dugan, William D.
Dugas, Wilson L.
Dolan, William H.

Farnum, Larry
Garrett, George R.
Graham, Jerome
Godbold, Earl P.
Granger, Paul
Grosser, Verner
Gudger, Troy
Hale, E.E.
Hettel, William
Hensing, Clarence
Howe, John
Hunter, Richard
Hubwer, Ernest
Jenner, Bill
Jackson, King
Johnson, Lester F.
McKay, Samuel
McMurray, Neal S.
Motiska, Stephen J.
Nix, Omer
Oberkiser, Earl
Patta, Glen
Paxton, William
Phillips, Vernon
Perkins, Donald E.
Pollack, Harry
Redden, Gene W. Lt. Col.
Richards, Jim
Reyna, Richard M.
Rooker, Jack
Rucker, Roy J.
Schneider, Bert
Sczsurek, Joe
Smith, Herschel R.
Smolka, John
Simon, William R.
Sandifed, Tom
Sims, George
Staples, Harold
Thompson, Charles
Tiffany, Andy
Vincent, George
Vossen, Harold
Weaver, Norman M.
Weaver, Willis W.
Webber, Jack C.
Wenzel, Clifford G.
West, Artis
Whitefield, James T.
Wiese, Fred W. Jr.
Wilson, Charles E.
Wlosek, Edmond J.
York, Harry J.
Zivic, John A.

Tributes To The Defense Battalions

Master Technical Sergeant Alvin M. Mosley, Jr.; a Ma combat correspondent wrote in 1944 that "since the beginn of the war many of the men...had seen action in units sma than divisions—in defense and raider battalions and other s cial commands." These Marines "had been fighting for a lo time," he said. Leather Neck, a magazine published by and f Marines, predicted in September 1944 that not until the wa was won would the complete story of each defense battalion b told. Because of the vital part they played, "much informatio about them...must be withheld, but there are no American troops with longer combat records in this war.

Defense battalion war diaries, muster rolls, and the unit files held by the Marine Corps historical center provide the basis for the following brief accounts of the service of the various defense battalions.

1st Defense Battalion

(November 1939-May 1944)

The Unit, formed at San Diego, California deployed to the Pacific as one of the Rainbow Five, the five defense battalions stationed there in accordance with the Rainbow 5 war plan when the Japanese attacked Pearl Harbor. Under Lt. Col. Bert A. Bone, elements of the battalion arrived in Hawaii in March 1941. The unit provided defense attachments for Johnston and Palmyra Islands in March and April of that year and for Wake Island in August. The Wake Island detachment of the 1st Defense Battalion received the Presidential unit citation for the defense of that outpost — which earned the nickname "Wake Island Defenders". Other elements dealt with hit-and-run raids at Palmyra and Johnston Islands in March 1942, the scattered detachments became Garrison Forces and a reconstituted battalion took shape in Hawaii. Command passes to Colonel Curtis W. LeGette in May 1942 and to Lt. Col. John H. Griebel in September. Lt. Col. Frank P. Hager exercised command briefly; his successor, Colonel Lewis H. Hohn, took the unit to Kwajalein and Eniwetok, in the Marshall Islands, in February 1944. The following month found the battalion in Majuro, also in the Marshalls, where it became the 1st antiaircraft artillery battalion on May 7, 1944. Under the command of Lt. Col. Jean H. Buckner as an antiaircraft unit. It served as part of the Guam Garrison, remaining on the Island through 1947.

artillery battalion on June 15, 1944. The organization was disbanded at Guadalcanal on the last day of that year.

4th Defense Battalion

(February 1940-May 1944)

The organization took shape at Parris Island, South Carolina under Major George F. Good, Jr.; Col. Lloyd L. Leech took over in April; and Lt. Col. Jesse L. Perkins in December 1940. February 1941 until deployed to defend Gutanamo Bay, Cuba. Battalion arrived under Col. Harold S. Fasset in the Pacific in time to become one of the Rainbow Five. Its strength was divided between Pearl Harbor and Midway, and helped defend both bases against Japanese attacks on December 7, 1941. March 1942 deployed to new hebrides and moved to New Zealand July 1943 then to Guadalcanal before landing in August 1943 at Vella Lavella in support of the 1st Marine amphibious corps. After becoming the 4th/AAA battalion on May 15, 1944, the unit returned to Guadalcanal in June but ended the war on Okinawa 4-45.

5th Defense Battalion

(December 1940-April 1944)

Organized at Parris Island, South Carolina, under Colonel Lloyd L. Leech, the 5th defense battalion subsequently became the 14th defense battalion, thus earning the unofficial title of 'Five: Fourteen'. Colonel Leech took the 5th defense battalion (minus the 5-artillery group) to Iceland with the Marine brigade sent there to relieve the British Garrison he brought the unit back to the United States in March 1942, and in July it sailed for the South Pacific, where one detachment set up its weapons at Noumea, New Caledonia, and another defended Tulagi in the Solomons after the 1st Marine division landed there in August 1942. The bulk of the battalion went to Ellis Island; there Colonel George F. Good, Jr. assumed command in November, and was relieved in December by Lt. Col. Willis E. Hicks. On January 16, 1943 the part of the unit located at Tulagi was redesignated the 14th defense battalion, while the remainder in the Ellis Group became the Marine defense force, Funafuti. In March 1944 it sailed for Hawaii where, on April 16, it became the 5th antiaircraft artillery battalion, seeing action under the designation during the latter stages of the Okinawa campaign.

6th Defense Battalion

(March 1941-February 1946)

Lt. Col. Charles I. Murray formed the battalion at San Diego, California; but turned it over to Col. Raphael Griffin, who took it to Hawaii in July 1941. It relieved the 3rd defense battalion at Midway in September. In June 1942, the 6th, now commanded by Lt. Col. Harold D. Shannon, helped fight of a Japanese air attack and repair bomb damage, thus earing a Navy unit commendation. The battalion remained at Midway until redesignated Marine Barracks, Naval base Midway, on February 1946. The wartime commanders who succeeded Shannon were Lieutenant Colonels Lewis A. Hohn, Rupert R. Deese, John H. Griebal, Charles T. Tingle, Frank P. Hager Jr.; Robert L. McKee, Herbert R. Nusbaum, and Wilfred Weaver and Major Robert E. Hommel.

7th Defense Battalion

(December 1940-April 1944)

Lt. Col. Lester A. Dessez formed the unit in San Diego, California, as a composite battalion of infantry and artillery. In March 1941, he took the outfit to Tutuila, Samoa, as one of the Rainbow Five. The 7th later deployed to Upola and established a detachment at Savaii. Colonel Curtis LeGette took command in December 1942, and in August of the following year, the battalion moved to Nanoumeain Ellice Islands in preparation for supporting operations against the Gilbert Islands. Lt. Col. Henry R. Paige took over in December 1943 and brought the unit to Hawaii where, on April 16, 1944, it became the 7th antiaircraft artillery battalion. As an antiaircraft outfit, it deployed to Anguar, Palau Islands, in September 1944, where it served as the Garrison force for the remainder of the war.

8th Defense Battalion

(April 1942-April 1944)

Lt. Col. Augusts W. Cockrell raised this battalion from units at Tutuila, Samoa. In May 1942, the battalion deployed to the Wallis Islands, were it was redesignated the Island Defense Force. Lt. Col. Earl Sneeringer assumed command for two weeks in August 1943. Before turning the unit over to Colonel Clyde H. Hartsel, Colonel Lloyd L. Leech became battalion commander in October 1943, a month before the unit deployed to Apamama in the Gilberts. On April 16, 1944, after moving to Hawaii, the organization became the 8th antiaircraft artillery battalion and as such, took part in the Okinawa campaign, remaining on the

Island until November 1945 when the Unit returned to the United States.

9th Defense Battalion

(February 1942-September 1944)

Formed at Parris Island, South Carolina and known as the "Fighting Ninth", the battalion was First Commanded by Major Wallace O. Thompson, who brought it to Cuba where it helped defend the Guantanamo Naval Base. Lt. Col. Bernard Dubel and his successor, Colonel David R. Nimmer, commanded the Battalion while it served in Cuba, and Nimmer remained in command when the Unit landed in November 1942 to reinforce the defenses of Guadalcanal. In preparation for further action, the Battalion emphasized mobility and artillery support of ground operations at the expense of its coastal defense mission. Lt. Col. William Scheyer commanded the 9th during the fighting in the Central Solomons. Here it set up antiaircraft guns and heavy artillery on Rendova to support the fighting on neighboring New Georgia before moving to New Georgia itself and deploying its light tanks and other weapons. The Battalion tanks also supported Army troops on Arundel Island. Lt. Col. Archie E. O'Neil was in command when the Unit landed at Guam on D-Day, July 21, 1944. The Battalion was awarded the Navy unit commendation for its service in action at Guadalcanal, Rendova, New Georgia, and Guam. Redesignated the 9th Antiaircraft Artillery Battalion in September 1944, the Unit returned to the United States in 1946.

10th Defense Battalion

(June 1942-May 1944)

Formed under Colonel Robert Blake at San Diego, California the Unit arrived in the Solomon Islands in February 1943, and participated in the Defense of Tulagi in that group and Banika in the Russell Islands. The Battalions light tanks saw action on New Georgia and nearby Arundel Island. Under Lieutenant Colonel Wallace O. Thompson who assumed command in July 1943, the 10th landed with the 22nd Marines at Eniwetok Atoll, Marshall Islands, in February 1944. Unit personnel are authorized to wear the Navy Unit Commendation Ribbon. Eniwetok Atoll was the first Japanese territory taken from the enemy by forces of the United Nations. The Unit was redesignated the 10th Antiaircraft Artillery Battalion on May 7, 1944.

11th Defense Battalion

(June 1942-May 1944)

This Battalion was activated at Parris Island, South Carolina, under Colonel Charles N. Muldrow and deployed during December 1942 to Efate in the New Hebrides. Beginning in January 1943, it helped defend Tulagi in the Solomons and Banika in the Russells Group. During the Central Solomons campaign it fought on Rendova, New Georgia, and Arundel Islands. In August, the entire Battalion came together on New Georgia and in March 1944 deployed the short distance to Arundel Island. Redesignated the 11th Antiaircraft Artillery Battalion on May 16, 1944, the Unit moved to Guadalcanal where it was deactivated same year.

12th Defense Battalion

(August 1942-June 1944)

Colonel William H. Harrison activated this Unit at San Diego, California; and took it to Hawaii in January 1943. After a brief stay in Australia, the 12th landed in June 1943 at Woodlark Island off New Guinea. Next the 12th took part in the assault on Cape Gloucester, New Britain in December 1943. Lt. Col. Merlyn D. Homes assumed command in February 1944, and on June 15, 1944 the Defense Battalion was redesignated the 12th Antiaircraft Artillery Battalion. It moved to the Russell Islands in June and in September to Peleliu, where it remained through 1945.

13th Defense Battalion

(September 1942-April 1944)

Colonel Bernard Dubel formed the Battalion at Guantanamo Bay, Cuba, where it defended the Naval Base throughout the war. In February 1944 Colonel Richard M. Cutts, Jr.; took command. The Unit became the 13th Antiaircraft Artillery Battalion on April 15 and was disbanded after the war.

14th Defense Battalion

(January 1943-September 1944)

Colonel Galen M. Sturgis organized this battalion from the elements of the 5th Defense Battalion on Tulagi, which inspired the nickname "Five:Fourteenth". Lt. Col. Jessie L. Perkins took command in June 1943 and during his tour of duty, the

Battalion operated on Tulagi and sent a detachment to Emirau, St. Mathias Islands, to support a landing there in March 1944. Lt. Col. William F. Parks took over from Perkins that same month and in April brought the unit to Guadalcanal to prepare for future operations. The organization landed at Guam in July and in September became the 14th Antiaircraft Artillery Battalion, remaining on the Island until after the war ended.

15th Defense Battalion

(October 1943-May 1944)

Organized in Hawaii by Lt. Col. Francis B. Loomis, Jr. from the 1st Airdome Battalion at Pearl Harbor, the Unit bore the nickname "First:Fifteenth". Beginning in January 1944, it served at Kwajalein and Majuro Atolls in the Marshalls Lt. Col. Peter J. Negri assumed command in May 1944, shortly before the Unit on the 7th of that month, became the 15th Antiaircraft Artillery Battalion.

16th Defense Battalion

(November 1942-April 1944)

Lt. Col. Richard P. Ross, Jr., formed the Unit on Johnston Island from elements of the 1st Defense Battalion that had been stationed there. Lt. Col. Bruce T. Hemphill took over in July 1943 and turned the Unit over to Lt. Col. August F. Penzold, Jr., in March of the following year. Redesignated the 16th Antiaircraft Artillery Battalion on April 19, 1944. The Outfit went to Hawaii by the end of August. It subsequently deployed to Tinian, remaining there until moving to okinawa in April 1945.

17th Defense Battalion

(March 1944-April 1944)

At Kauai in Hawaii, Lt. Col. Thomas G. McFarland organized this Unit from the 2nd Airdome Battalion, which had returned form duty in the Ellice Islands. The redesignation gave rise to the nickname "Two:Seventeen", and the motto "One of a Kind". On April 19, the Defense Battalion became the 17th Antiaircraft Artillery Battalion. It moved to Saipan in July and to Tinian in August. At the Latter Island, it provided antiaircraft defense for both Tinian Town and North Field, form which B-29s took off with the atomic bombs that leveled Hiroshima and Nagasaki.

18th Defense Battalion

(October 1943-April 1944)

Activated at New River, North Carolina, by Lt. Col. Harold C. Roberts, who was replaced in January 1944 by Lt. Col. William C. Van Ryzin, the Unit became the 18th Antiaircraft Artillery Battalion on May 16, 1944 by August, Echelons of the Battalion were located at Saipan and Tinian, but by September it had come together on the Latter Island, where it remained until the end of the war.

51st Defense Battalion

(August 1942-January 1946)

Organized at Mondford Point Camp, New River, North Carolina, this was the first of two Defense Battalions commanded by white officers, but organized from among African-American Marines who had trained at Montford Point. Colonel Samuel Woods Jr., who commanded the Mondfort Point Camp, formed the Battalion and became its first commanding officer. Lt. Col. William B. Onley took over in March 1943 and Lt. Col. Floyd A. Stephenson in April. The initial plan called for the 51st to be a composite Unit with the Infantry and Pack Howitzer Elements, but in June 1943 it became a conventional Defense Battalion. Lt. Col. Curtis W. LeGette assumed command in January 1944 and took the Battalion to Nanoumea and Funafuti in the Ellice Islands, where it arrived by the end of February 1944. In September, the 51st deployed to Eniwetok in the Marshalls where, in December, Lt. Col. Gould P. Groves became Battalion Commander, a post he held throughout the rest of the war. In June 1945, Lt. Col. Groves dispatched a composite group to provide antiaircraft defense for Kawajalein Atoll. The Battalion sailed from the Marshalls in November 1945 and disbanded at Montford Point in January 1946.

52nd Defense Battalion

(December 1943-May 1946)

This Unit like the 51st, was organized at Montfort, New River, North Carolina, and manned by African-Americans commanded by white officers. Planned as a composite Unit, the 52nd took shape as a conventional Defense Battalion. It absorbed the Pack Howitzer Crews made surplus when the 51st lost its composite status and retrained them in the employment of other weapons. Colonel Augustus W. Cockrell organized the unit, which he turned over to Lieutenant Colonel Joseph W.

Ernshaw in July 1944. Under Ernshaw, the 52nd the Unit deployed to the Marshalls, arriving in October to man the Antiaircraft Defenses of Majuro Atoll and Roi-Namur in Kwajalein Atoll. Lt. Col. David W. Silvey assumed command in January 1945, and between March and May the entire Battalion deployed to Guam, remaining there for the rest of the war. Lt. Col. Thomas C. Moore Jr. replaced Silvey in May 1945, and in November, the 52nd relieved the 51st at Kwajalein and Eniwetok Atolls before returning to Medford Point; where it became the 3rd Antiaircraft Artillery Battalion (composite).

****

Available in the archives at the Marine Corps Historical Center is an impressive body of primary source material prepared by individual Defense Battalions during the Pacific War. Also in the Marine Corps Historical Center are the oral history and personal paper collections, containing many first-hand accounts of World War II. Major Charles D. Melson (Ret.) 1967-1992

****

Major General Charles D. Barrett while a Colonel, together with Lt. Col. Robert H. Pepper, played a major role in the development of the Defense Battalion.

Marine Corps Defense Battalions could operate as integral units in support of a base or Beachhead, positioning their weapons and equipment to cover assigned sectors and meet specific threats.

Because a Defense Battalion could, in effect, form task organizations, it somewhat resembled the large infantry regiment, which could employ battalion combat teams. According to Lieutenant Heinl, in terms of "Strength and variety of material, "The Defense Battalion" might well be a regiment. With the Seacoast and Antiaircraft Artillery Groups are almost small battalions, while the other three separate batteries (search light and sound locator and the two machine gun units) are undeniable batteries in the accepted sense of the word."

Every Marine in a typical defense battalion had to train to fight as an infantryman in an emergency, with the members of gun and search light crews leaving their usual battle stations.

Although the armament of the typical wartime unit consisted of eight 155mm guns, twelve 90mm guns, nineteen 40mm guns, twenty-eight 20mm guns and 35 .50-caliber heavy machine guns, re-enforced in some instances by eight M3 light tanks.

Defense Battalions deployed early and often throughout the Pacific campaigns, serving in distant, dangerous and endured isolation, sickness, many months of primitive living conditions for the task of protecting advance bases in less than attractive tropical paradises.

Master Technical Sergeant Alvin M. Jospehy, Jr., a Marine Combat Correspondent, wrote in 1944 that "since the beginning of the war many of the men...had seen action in units smaller than divisions—in Defense and Raider Battalions and other special commands." These Marines "had been fighting for a long period of time," he said. Leathernick, a magazine published by and for Marines, predicted in September 1944 that not until the war won would the complete story of each Defense Battalion be told. Because of the vital part they played," much information about them...must be withheld, BUT THERE ARE NO AMERICAN TROOPS WITH LONGER COMBAT RECORDS IN THIS WAR.

To Be A Marine

Maybe my advancing years have caused me to become more poetic, more sentimental, or maybe, more psychotic; but the most impressive item of yesterday's pageant was an old man standing in the background in civilian clothes, watching the events unfold on the parade field. I notice him and tried to ignore him. But I couldn't. My eyes kept going back to him. He must have been in his early sixties. He had a weathered look of a retired Marine. I kept looking at him and I saw a much more meaningful scene unfold on his face and in his eyes as he watched the ceremony. I saw a lifetime of dedication and loyalty. I saw the deep love he felt for the Marine Corps. I saw the blind obedience of a young recruit for the mere utterances of his NCOs. I saw the pride of a young Marine on his first leave as he strutted about in his uniform. I saw the fear of battle well controlled by the discipline seemingly inherent in him. I saw the sorrow of lost comrades. I saw the bravery which caused him to wade ashore on countless beaches in the face of murderous fire. I saw the strength and hope that caused him to suffer defeat and withstand imprisonment. I saw the humanity that precluded rage and long-lasting hate for the enemy who had tried to kill him in so many wars. I saw the frustrations of dozens of barriers thrown before him as he tried to do his job with the furious dedication of a truly professional Marine. I saw the love for his family and the hope for his children. I saw the heartbreak of the realization that he was alone. But through it all, I saw the overwhelming love, reflected in his moist eyes, for the Marine Corps and all it stood for. I felt humbled in his presence.

I wanted to talk with him when the ceremony ended, but all I could say as I passed him was, "Happy Birthday, Marine."

Excerpt from *Green Side Out*, By Major Gene Duncan, 1978

PACIFIC THEATER CASUALTIES

BATTLE DEATHS

BY CAMPAIGN

Campaigns are listed in order of highest ground combat deaths.

MARINE CORPS

Campaign	Dates	Battles Deaths	Percent of Total
Iwo Jima	19 Feb.-26 March 1945	5,931	26.3%
Okinawa	1 April-22 June 1945	3,443	15.3%
Saipan	11 June-10 July 1944	3,152	14.0%
Guam	21 July-15 Aug. 1944	1,568	6.9%
Guadalcanal	7 Aug. 1942-8 Feb. 1943	1,504	6.6%
Peleliu	6 Sept.-14 Oct. 1944	1,336	5.9%
Tarawa	20 Nov.-8 Dec. 1943	1,085	4.8%
Solomons-New Britain (Air)	9 Feb. 1943-15 March 1945	783	3.4%
Bougainville	28 Oct. 1943-15 June 1944	732	3.2%
Bataan/Corregidor	7 Dec. 1941-6 May 1942	570	2.5%
Cape Gloucester	26 Dec. 1943-1 March 1944	438	1.9%
Kwaialein/Maiuro	29 Jan.-8 Feb. 1944	387	1.7%
Tinian	24 July-1 Aug. 1944	368	1.6%
Eniwetok	17 Feb.-2 March 1944	258	1.1%
Sea Duty (Naval Battles)	7 Dec. 1941-2 Sept. 1945	242	1.0%
New Georgia	20 June-16 Oct. 1943	221	*All the remainder less than 1%*
Marshalls, Carolines, Palau, Philippines Volcano and Bonin Islands (Air)	Feb. 1944-June 1945	200	
Wake Atoll	7-23 Dec. 1941	69	
Gilberts, Marshalls, Marianas (Air)	Nov. 1943-Aug. 1944	65	
Midway Islands	7 Dec. 1941-6 June 1942	48	
Talasea (New Britain)	6 March 1944	37	
Makin (Gilberts)	17-18 Aug. 1942	30	
Guam (Marianas)	7-10 Dec. 1941	10	
Arawe, Russell Is. Treasury Island	1943-1944	2	
Total		**22,479***	

1st Marine Div.

4th Marine Div.

2nd Marine Div.

5th Marine Div.

3rd Marine Div.

6th Marine Div.

GROUND CASUALTIES

BY DIVISION

MARINE CORPS

Division	Combat Deaths	Wounded in Action
1st Marine	3,470	14,438
4th Marine	3,345	12,045
2nd Marine	2,795	9,975
5th Marine	2,414	7,159
3rd Marine	2,371	8,045
6th Marine	1,630	7,700
Total	**16,025**	**59,362**

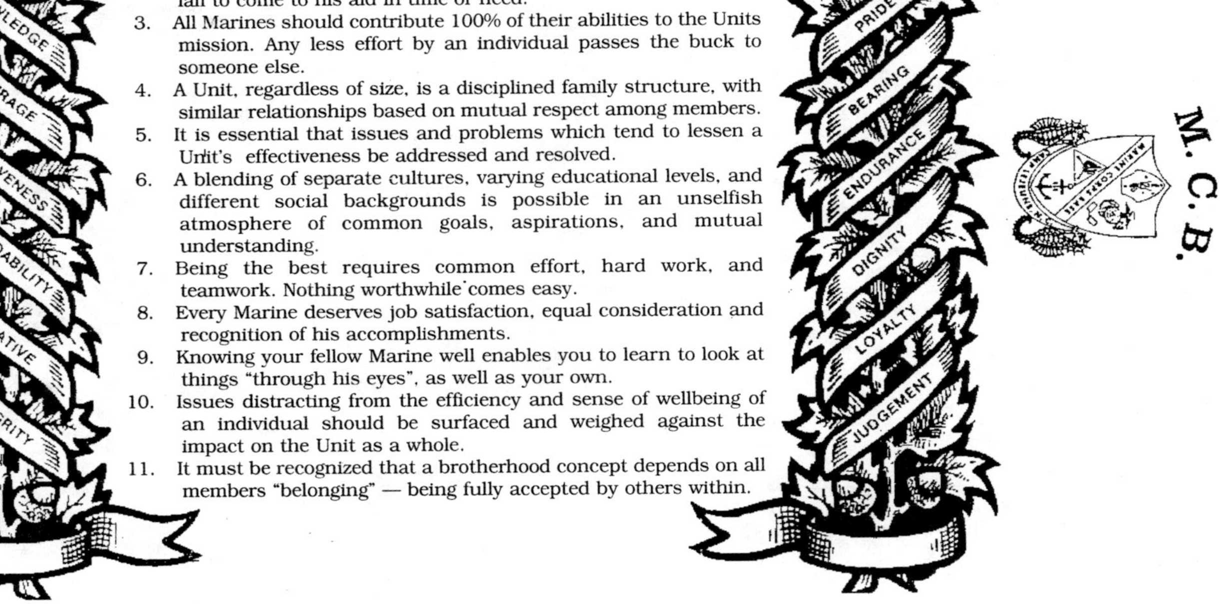

BAND OF BROTHERS

1. All Marines are entitled to dignity and respect as individuals, but must abide by common standards established by proper authority.
2. A Marine should never lie, cheat, or steal form a fellow Marine or fail to come to his aid in time or need.
3. All Marines should contribute 100% of their abilities to the Units mission. Any less effort by an individual passes the buck to someone else.
4. A Unit, regardless of size, is a disciplined family structure, with similar relationships based on mutual respect among members.
5. It is essential that issues and problems which tend to lessen a Unit's effectiveness be addressed and resolved.
6. A blending of separate cultures, varying educational levels, and different social backgrounds is possible in an unselfish atmosphere of common goals, aspirations, and mutual understanding.
7. Being the best requires common effort, hard work, and teamwork. Nothing worthwhile comes easy.
8. Every Marine deserves job satisfaction, equal consideration and recognition of his accomplishments.
9. Knowing your fellow Marine well enables you to learn to look at things "through his eyes", as well as your own.
10. Issues distracting from the efficiency and sense of wellbeing of an individual should be surfaced and weighed against the impact on the Unit as a whole.
11. It must be recognized that a brotherhood concept depends on all members "belonging" — being fully accepted by others within.

ORDER FORM

"HEROES UNDER THE BIG DIPPER"

AS TOLD BY AUTHOR PETER LA CIVITA

QTY	ITEM	COST PER	TOTAL
	HEROES UNDER THE BIG DIPPER	$12.95	
Add $3 PER BOOK SHIPPING & HANDLING		$ 3.00	
PA. RES. ADD 7.0% SALES TAX PER BOOK			
		TOTAL	

Name____

Address______________________________________

City ____________________ State______ Zip__________

Fill out and send this order form with payment to:

BRYANMARC BOOKS
Box 154
East McKeesport, PA 15035